Golden Highlights Library

Early Airplanes

John Blake

Camden House Books

Camden House Books
Printed and published by BPCC Publishers
Manufactured under licence from the proprietor

Created, designed and produced by
Trewin Copplestone Publishing Ltd, London

Made and printed in Great Britain by
Purnell and Sons (Book Production) Ltd.,
Member of the BPCC Group, Paulton, Bristol

ISBN 0 905015 06 1

Acknowledgments

Photographs were provided by the following:
Air Portraits Colour Library: 21, 32, 36t, 45tl, tr;
John Blake: 70–1; Boeing Company: 78, 79; Culver
Pictures Inc: 14, 18–19; Michael Dyer Associates: 12t,
13t, 16t, 17bl, 28, 39, 40, 47, 48, 49b, 51, 52t, 53t, b,
55b, 56, 57, 59t, 64, 65t, 67, 72, 73t, 74b, 75, 77t;
Flight International: 13b, 25, 26, 27b, 34t, 35b, 38,
66t, 70t; Thomas G. Foxworth 73b; Charles Gibbs-
Smith: 3; James Gilbert: 1, 36b, 37, 65b; Imperial
War Museum, London: 19, 41t, b, 43t, b, 44, 45b,
46t, b, 50–1, 52b, 55t; London Transport: 24r;
Lufthansa: 59b, 74t; National Air and Space Museum,
Smithsonian Institution: 17br; Radio Times Hulton
Picture Library: 11t, b, 22; Real Photographs: 54;
Royal Aeronautical Society: 18, 23t, b, 27t, 35t, 42,
69b; Science Museum, London: 4, 6, 7, 9, 10, 12b, 20,
24l, United Service and Royal Aero Club: 15t, b, 30b,
50, 58, 62–63, 62b, 63b, 70b; US Navy: 31.
The publishers also gratefully acknowledge:
Leonard Bridgman: 72; Trewin Copplestone
Publishing: 5, 8, 17t, 29, 32–3, 48b, 70t, 76–7, 80;
Leach Corporation "Heritage of the Air Collection:"
40, 49, 53t, b, 56; Kenneth McDonough 77; National
Aviation Museum, Ottawa 57; National Museum of
Science and Technology, Ottawa: 16t, 28; Phillips
Petroleum Company: 77t, 30t; Royal Air Force
Museum, Hendon: 12t, 13t; Editions SERMA, Paris:
52t; Brian Withams: 49b.

Contents

Page 1 *The Shuttleworth Trust in England
operate this last flying example of the Bristol
Fighter.*

Cayley's own drawing, in plan form, of his 1799 aircraft – the world's first modern-looking aircraft. The drawing shows the cruciform tail unit, but not the propulsive paddles.

Sir George Cayley

BORN in 1773, Sir George Cayley has been called "the true inventor of the airplane" and "the father of English aviation." Some of the discoveries that he successfully applied and subsequently published had already been described or introduced by others, such as his successful helicopter model of 1796, based on the work of Launoy and Bienvenu in Paris twelve years earlier. However, most of his work was original and he is famous chiefly for his considerable achievement of being the man who first set down clearly all the requirements for the modern airplane.

He defined the basic problem as being "to make a surface support a given weight by the application of power to the resistance of the air," and in sketches and descriptions he showed a monoplane with cambered wing surface, separate moveable control surfaces at the tail and – for the first time in history – the power unit divorced from the lifting unit. This meant, in other words, a wing to provide lift and an engine (in this case flapping surfaces) to provide thrust.

Cayley constructed successful models to test and prove his basic theory of flight; he invented numerous details found in later aircraft, such as the bicycle-type tension-wheel undercarriage, and he explored and formulated all the basic aerodynamic requirements for controlled flight. He grasped the fact that separate, adjustable tail controls were necessary for successful flight, and he also appreciated the value of a cambered wing surface for lift.

He flew a full-sized glider monoplane in 1809, and triplanes in 1849 and 1853, on the last occasion making the first brief manned flight in history.

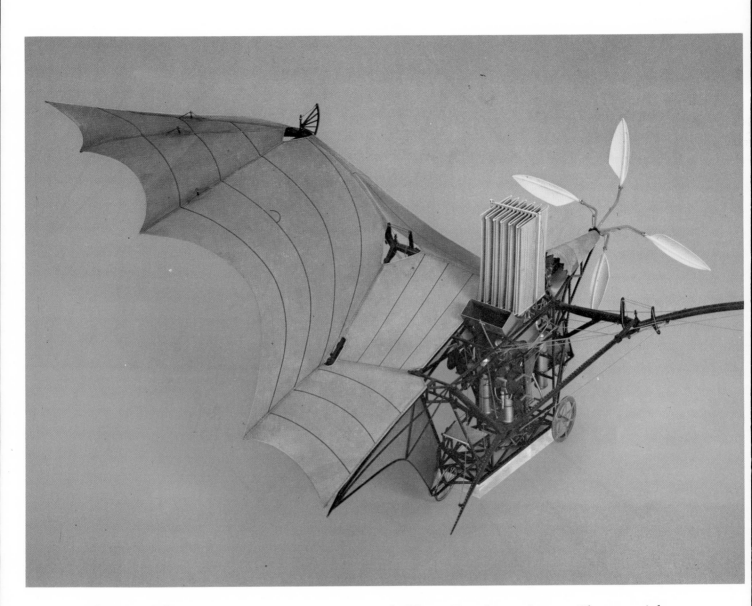

Clement Ader

WHILE Cayley had conceived a practical theoretical engine and had successfully flown three gliders, he could go no further because he lacked a power unit—although in a paper of 1809 he set out the first-ever description for an internal combustion aircraft engine. No such engine was to appear, however, for nearly 100 years, and in the interval the experimenters were forced to turn to other sources of power, such as steam and electricity.

Both were successfully applied to lighter-than-air craft, where lift was abundant, but the engines of the 19th century were, with one exception, far too heavy and bulky for use in a heavier-than-air machine. The margin of lift over weight was—when it existed in early experiments at all—far too slight for the boilers or batteries of such engines.

The exception came from the brain of a brilliant French engineer, Clement Ader. Born in 1841, he began his practical experiments in aviation with a tethered glider in 1873, starting work on a powered aircraft which he called *Eole* nine years later. To power it he designed and built his own steam engine that was a masterpiece, producing 20 hp for a total weight, including boiler and accessories, of 112 lb. As the aircraft, with pilot, weighed only 653 lb, this gave a wing loading of a mere 2 lb per square foot, and a power loading of 33 lb per horsepower.

Eole, apart from its exceptional power plant, featured an airscrew made of bamboo "feathers" such that the pitch would have progressively flattened from the tip under increasing load, providing an automatic pitch-change control very similar to that achieved with metal blades on some modern racing aircraft. Ader also provided mechanisms for sweeping the wings forward or back, in-

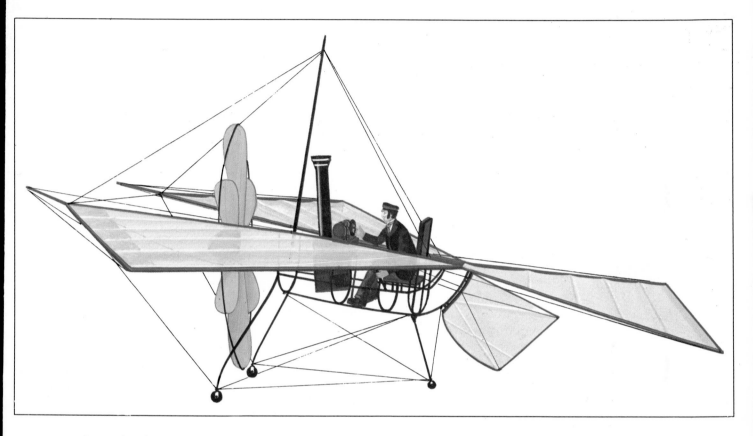

dependently, to adjust the center of pressure, for changing the area and the camber, and for flexing the tips. This incredibly complex arrangement of ribs and struts, operated by cords and pulleys, designed to provide control in flight, was based on the wing structure and operating methods of the bat. Why, in the face of common sense and of much published material favoring simpler methods of control, Ader clung to this bat mechanism, is one of the mysteries of aviation. It may well have been sheer romanticism—the bat is the only true flying mammal—but cannot have been based on very knowledgeable study. Even today, the bat's means of achieving control over its own wings is obscure.

On October 9, 1890, at about four o'clock in the afternoon, in the grounds of a château at Armainvilliers, Ader, then forty-nine years of age, achieved the first powered takeoff from level ground in history, being airborne for about 165 feet. The smallness of the prepared ground and the evident lack of stability of the machine forbade further tests and Ader returned to the drawing board.

His second aircraft, *Avion II,* was abandoned before completion. (Ader coined the word "avion" as a general word for aircraft.) *Avion III* was tested twice at Satory in October, 1897. It was damaged on the second test, and no further attempts were made. Military funds had been provided to enable Ader to complete *Avion III,* and General Mensier witnessed the attempts and wrote an official report.

Although that report denied that the *Avion* had ever left the ground, nine years later, faced by the success of others, Ader was to claim that he had flown for nearly 1000 ft on the second test on October 14. All the contemporary evidence points to this being totally untrue.

It was this fragile-looking tailed glider of Lilienthal's, combined with the Hargrave box kite, that was to result in the definitive biplane.

Lilienthal, Pilcher and Chanute

WHILE the developments of such men as Cayley, Ader, du Temple and Mozhaisky in Russia, who launched a full-scale steam-powered monoplane from a ramp in 1884, provided the first gropings towards sustained flight, there existed an almost universal ignorance of how to control any aircraft that achieved it. Although Cayley discovered the secret and published his findings, and du Temple proposed tail surfaces for his aircraft, neither Ader nor Mozhaisky, nor Sir Hiram Maxim, an American turned Briton who experimented in Kent with a vast, steam-powered aircraft weighing $3\frac{1}{2}$ tons, could ever have controlled their monsters in the air.

Considerable progress had been made during this period with powered models. Pénaud flew a rubber-powered model in France in 1871 and his fellow-countryman, Tatin, a twin-propeller model powered by compressed air in 1879. In 1893 Hargrave, the inventor of the box kite, was flying powered models in Australia, and Langley, in the United States, achieved success with two steam-powered model aircraft in 1896. Adequate, light power for full-sized machines, however, was still lacking.

Three very important men now come upon the scene: in Germany, Otto Lilienthal; in Britain, Percy Pilcher; in the United States, Octave Chanute. Led by Lilienthal, they grasped the principle that only by constant practice could they master their machine, and because they had no engines they turned to gliding.

Lilienthal commenced his flying in 1891, following two earlier unsuccessful designs, with a monoplane with a cruciform tail to give stability in pitch and yaw. Fifteen further designs followed.

He died following a crash in 1896—the first man to be killed testing an aircraft as he was the first to achieve sustained flight in one.

Lilienthal never achieved powered flight, although he prepared for it and installed, but never used, a carbonic acid motor in some of his gliders. His achievements, however, make him one of the key figures in the history of flying. The first man to remain in the air long enough to claim controlled flight (his longest glide was 750 feet), he was, at the time of his death, beginning to experiment with moveable controls, although most of his machines

were controlled to a very limited degree simply by movements of the pilot's body to shift the center of gravity.

Lilienthal wrote extensively of his technical findings and experiments, and the widespread publication of these writings inspired both Pilcher, a young Scotsman, and Chanute. Pilcher built and flew four monoplane gliders, based on Lilienthal's designs, and by the time of his death in 1899 – also in a crash – had built and tested an engine for a powered version. Had he lived, he might well have anticipated the Wrights, as his flying was based on sound principles.

Chanute, an older man who took up glider designing at the age of sixty-four, also owed much to Lilienthal, and perfected the biplane glider invented by the German. He also wrote widely in technical journals, and was responsible for bringing Lilienthal's work to public notice in America, in particular to the Wright brothers, whose friend and supporter he was.

Below *In the 19th century Lawrence Hargrave established the rigid truss structure that was the basis of all successful biplanes.*

Below *Something of the feeling of Victorian engineers for economy and grace in mechanical construction appears in Sir Hiram Maxim's huge steam aircraft. Here it is tethered to a thrust-measuring rig.*

The Wright Brothers

WITH the mass of information that had been recorded the stage was set, with the introduction of the internal combustion engine, for the achievement of true powered flight by the Wright brothers, Wilbur and Orville.

The true stature of the Wright brothers is measured by three achievements. They designed, built and flew the first practical powered aircraft in the world; they correctly analyzed and applied the coordinated control movements necessary to handle an aircraft in the air; and they were the catalyst that set off the great European burgeoning in aircraft design and performance in the period between 1908 and 1910.

Inspired by Lilienthal and encouraged by Chanute, the brothers began successful gliding experiments in 1900. By 1903 they were ready with their first powered aircraft, and on December 17 at Kitty Hawk, N.C., they made four flights; the longest – and last – was of 825 feet. These were the first sustained powered airplane flights in the world.

It had not been easy. Although the internal combustion four-stroke engine had been in use in automobiles since at least 1875, the Wrights found none reliable or light enough for their purpose and so designed their own engine which developed a scant 25 hp from its four cylinders.

The theory of airscrews had been known since the 15th century, and models powered by them were in use in the 19th. (Curiously,

Cayley totally ignored the airscrew after his first model helicopter.) But the published data were inadequate and mostly inaccurate, so the Wrights (who also built their own wind tunnel) started from scratch and designed their own airscrews. By 1905, with their third aircraft, they were capable of maneuvering in flight, and Wilbur flew over 24 miles in it on October 5. And still, amazingly, no one was interested. The Wrights made no secret of their flights and they were well known locally, but overtures to their own and other governments failed, and the press, except for garbled and uninformed reports from time to time, was silent. This universal indifference caused the brothers to abandon practical work for three years, although research continued. And then, in 1908, the situation changed dramatically.

The Wrights' Flyer emerged in May, modified to take two people, now sitting upright instead of prone as in earlier models. On May 14 the first-ever passenger flights took place; in September, the army purchased a Flyer. Most important of all, between August 8, 1908, and May 31, 1909, the brothers demonstrated a similar aircraft in France, giving passenger flights and instruction. Progress in Europe had slowed to a snail's pace after the first tentative flights in 1906–1907; the effortless ease of maneuver shown by the big Wright biplane was an eye-opener, and shook the French out of their lethargy and complacency.

After this triumph of giving controlled flight to the world, their progress virtually ceased. Wilbur died in 1912, and although the last design came out in 1915 it contributed nothing to progress. By 1910, in fact, the rest of the field had outpaced them, and the hundred or so simple, popular, basic Flyers were becoming obsolete.

Far left *The Wright Flyer of 1903 was the prototype of all successful aircraft. Launched off a rail, like nearly all the Wright aircraft, it lacked the clumsy catapult of later Flyers. Painting by John Young.*

Below *The launching derrick with its concrete weight and cable fatally inhibited any real development of the Wright design.*

Langley's clumsy-looking tandem monoplane of 1903, developed from successful models like this, never actually flew.

Langley and Ferber

A very curious incident arose concerning a potential rival to the Wrights, Professor Samuel Pierpont Langley. Langley was an astronomer and mathematician, born in Roxbury, Mass., in 1834, who had interested himself in aeronautics at the age of fifty-three and after many failures succeeded in flying a series of powered models. Finally, in 1903, the same year that saw the first flight by the Wrights, he completed his full-size aircraft, the large and unwieldy *Aerodrome A*.

Langley lacked the simple, direct response of the Wrights to problems, and seemed to approach the solution to flight with Ptolemaic intricacy. His big, complex, tandem-wing monoplane, powered by a most advanced and effective radial engine, was launched by a complicated catapult from the roof of a houseboat and fitted with floats for a water landing. The pilot was his assistant Charles Manley, who had designed the engine, basing it on an earlier, unsuccessful Balzer rotary that Langley had ordered.

Manley had no piloting experience, and no tests had been made in gliding flight before the first attempt on October 7, 1903. Fouling the catapult, the *Aerodrome* crashed into the river. On December 8, less than a week before the Wrights' first flight at Kitty Hawk, the second and final test came to an identical end.

Langley had been financed by the War Department to the extent of $50,000 (urged on by President McKinley himself) and the failure of the two tests put an end to official support and almost certainly contributed to the notably cool reception of the War Department to the Wrights' overtures two years later.

And there the matter should have rested, but it did not. For in March 1914 the Smithsonian Institution contracted with Glenn Curtiss, one of the earliest American pioneers of aviation, to reconstruct and test the 1903 Langley *Aerodrome*. On May 28 and June 2, 1914, it flew successfully on Lake Keuka, N.Y., using a new set of floats and with the original engine. The Smithsonian published a statement that the *Aerodrome* was the first heavier-than-air machine capable of maintaining sustained human flight. As a result, in 1928, Dr. Orville Wright, in protest, sent the original Flyer to England.

In 1942 the Institute admitted that apart from the fitting of new floats major modifications had been carried out by Curtiss (who was an unsuccessful defendant in a patent case brought against him by the Wrights), and agreed to the latter's prior claim to flight. The logic of this whole attempt by a scientific body is baffling.

In Europe five years after Lilienthal's death a solitary French pioneer, Captain Ferber, was experimenting with similar gliders. Through Chanute, he learned enough of the Wrights' progress in gliding to copy them, though with little success. In 1904, he was to introduce the definitive pattern for European aircraft, an inherently stable, tailed glider on which he carried the first flying passenger the same year.

Ferber's contribution was vital, and eventually this type of inherently stable aircraft was to oust the unstable Wright Flyers that needed constant attention to keep them steady.

Right *Captain Ferber of the French Army. Military regulations forced him to appear at flying meetings under a pseudonym.*

Below *Captain Ferber built seven gliders and four powered aircraft; No. VI A, shown here on a test rig, was powered by a 6-hp Buchet motor but never flew.*

Engine Development

WRITING in Jane's *All the World's Aircraft* for 1919, the late Captain W. H. Sayers (RAF), said: "The development of the aeroplane has always waited upon the development of its source of motive power." This basic truth continued to be valid through most of the period covered in this book, when airplanes were more often than not underpowered. Many promising designs failed for lack of a suitable engine, and many of the most successful aircraft owed that success to the almost accidental availability of a powerful and reliable motor.

The Wrights, as we have seen, designed and built their own engine in 1903. A typical Wright solution, it contained much advanced thinking, including extensive use of light alloys. Nevertheless they left some very basic design where there seemed no good reason to spend time on refinement—such as the automatic inlet valves and crude surface carburetor. Power output varied between 25 and 12 hp, the engine overheating after a few minutes' operation. With this engine the Wrights flew, whereas Manley, in the Langley *Aerodrome*, with his own engine, did not, though the Manley–Balzer five-cylinder radial was more sophisticated than the Wright engine.

Manley introduced cast-iron liners to the cylinders, invented the system of a master connecting rod on which all subsequent radial engines are based, and seems to have been the first man to use a high-tension coil and distributor. Moreover his engine developed some 50 hp and held that power over extended runs, the longest of which was ten hours.

All the early experimenters employed original engines, but none were as effective as the Manley. The first successful production engines, enabling something like steady progress in flight to be made, came from France. Léon Levasseur, a builder of boat engines, turned to aviation in 1907 with a beautiful V8, water-cooled engine of 50 hp. Advanced in conception, with fuel injectors and evaporative cooling, it was very reliable and extremely light, weighing only 4.2 lb per hp. Nevertheless, it was not Levasseur's Antoinette but another engine, the Gnôme, that largely powered the great leaping advance of European aviation in the 1908–1910 "golden age."

Designed by the Séguin brothers in France, the Gnôme was not the first rotary, but it was incontestably the most successful. Unlike the radial, in the rotary engine the hollow crank-

The Gnôme rotary was built in several versions— this early 50-hp one, and later models of 70, 100 and 140 hp.

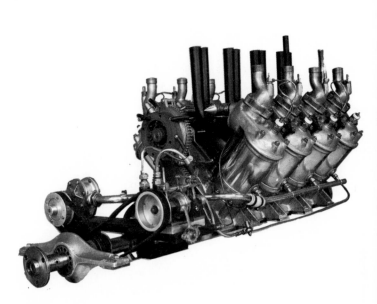

The first aircraft to fly in Britain was powered by one of Léon Levasseur's excellent V8 Antoinette engines, developed from his very successful marine units. From 1908 it was used in many European designs.

shaft was fixed and the cylinders whirled around it, providing adequate cooling in an age when all other engines ran too hot. Fuel and air were fed haphazardly to the inlet valves, set in the piston head, through the crankshaft. One result of this crude carburetion was to discourage the use of the throttle, control being effected by switching on and off. This crudity and the gyroscopic loads, which became enormous in later more powerful rotaries, eventually put it out of favor, but it survived until the end of the First World War.

In-line engines were developed alongside the rotary with vee arrangements, such as the Renault and single-line, water-cooled fours and sixes, much favored by the Germans. Power stayed around the 50–100 hp mark, the main improvements in the years between 1909 and 1914 being in detail design and cooling.

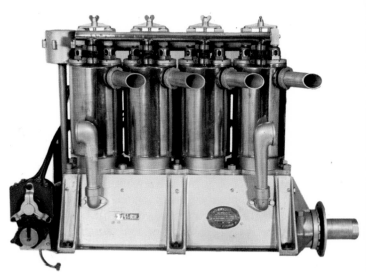

F. M. Green, a brilliant British engine designer, built this water-cooled, upright in-line engine. In various forms it powered many early aircraft and was the first to have enclosed overhead cam-valve gear, crankcase-lubricated.

This shot of the Green engine mounted in the nose of an Avro Type D biplane shows the simplicity of pioneer construction. Ease of maintenance and cooling problems dictated the exposed position.

More Pioneers

APART from the Wright brothers, no practical activity took place in the United States until 1908, when the first of Glenn Curtiss' designs, the *June Bug,* made a flight of over 5000 ft, winning the *Scientific American* prize for the first public flight in the United States to cover more than a kilometer.

Curtiss had been associated with three other successful aircraft that year built by the Aerial Experiment Association, of which he was the overall director of design. He also designed the 40-hp water-cooled engine that powered them all, and he produced a 50-hp V8 in 1908. (Charles Manley was employed by Curtiss for a time.)

A second V8 powered the Curtiss *Golden Flyer,* on which he flew 30 km in 24 minutes 15 seconds at the great Rheims meeting in 1909. In 1910 this type, a pusher biplane, became the standard Curtiss product and achieved fame with a number of cross-country flights in the United States. The following year saw the emergence of his first flying boat, the first successful seaplane in the world and the parent of a number of future Curtiss designs.

The link between Curtiss and naval flying was forged when Eugene Ely used one of his standard pushers in the first flight from a ship's deck, taking off from a platform on the cruiser USS *Birmingham.*

While this was happening in the United States, events had begun to move in Britain. After the death of Pilcher and the failure of Maxim's experiments at the end of the 19th century, nothing happened until 1908. In that year the first British pilots who had trained in France, such as J. T. C. Moore-Brabazon, returned, and the Short brothers negotiated a license to build Wright Flyers, setting up the first production line at Leysdown on the island of Sheppey.

Third of the four designs built by the Aerial Experiment Association, the June Bug, *flown by Glenn Curtiss, won the* Scientific American *Trophy for the first public flight in the USA on July 4, 1908.*

While there were at this period (1908) serious experimenter-designers like Samuel Franklin Cody and A. V. Roe, of whom more will be said later, the majority of the British pioneers were amateur sportsmen, and flying became more of a social pastime than in France. There, true to the national bent for scientific experiment that gave them the lead with automobiles, the French led the Europeans in aeronautical progress, so that the best British pilots "flew French" and British designs were very few.

An exception were the six owners who had bought the Short-built Wright Flyers. The most prominent of the six was the Hon. Charles Rolls, co-founder of Rolls-Royce and a convert to heavier-than-air from a passionate attachment to ballooning.

One of the leaders of the small band of British owner-pilots, Rolls was faithful to the Wright design (he had had an unsuccessful glider built by Shorts on the basis of descriptions of the Wright machine). Later, in 1910, he was killed on a French-built Wright with a modified tail.

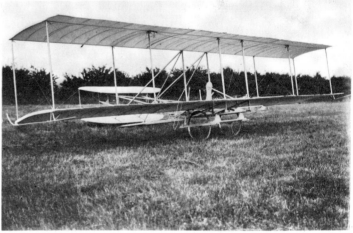

Above *Before he bought his powered Wright Flyers, Rolls had Short Brothers in England build him this rough copy of a Wright glider. It was not successful.*

Top *Charles Rolls made the first double, non-stop English Channel crossing on June 2, 1910, on this Wright A with flotation bags on the undercarriage.*

The Silver Dart, the fourth and last Aerial Experiment Association powered aircraft, was designed by James McCurdy and flown by him *and Baldwin. It had a 50-hp Curtiss motor. Painting by R. W. Bradford.*

The Channel Flight

MONOPLANE and biplane developed side by side, there being much to recommend each, but although the monoplane had shown itself to be as efficient and reliable as the biplane, it was the latter that dominated the scene. This was partly because of the latter's greater rigidity, simplicity and lightness, but it was also due in some measure to the greater popularity of one or two biplane types and a degree of quite unreasonable prejudice following a few monoplane structural failures.

Nevertheless it was a monoplane that was to make the first spectacular overwater flight. Léon Levasseur, the designer of the Antoinette engines, also built, for the firm of Gastambide et Mengin, a series of slender, graceful and efficient aircraft. The Antoinettes, the largest and heaviest of the monoplanes, had a span of 46 feet, the wings· being 10 feet in chord at the root. The steel, two-bladed propeller was driven at about 1100 rpm.

Weighing some 1045 lb, the Antoinette was more than twice the weight of its principal rival monoplane, the Blériot. Typical of all Louis Blériot's designs, the Type XI weighed 462 lb without the pilot and had a three-cylinder, 25-hp Anzani engine, driving a wooden propeller at 1200 rpm.

One event, which must count among the great moments of aviation, decided that the Blériot, not the Antoinette, would become the most popular monoplane. In 1908 the London *Daily Mail* had offered £500 for the first flight across the English Channel. Since there were no takers, it repeated the offer and doubled the money the following year.

In the summer of 1909 several well-known pilots were preparing for the flight, tempted by the prize money and by a further sum which had been on offer from the champagne industry since 1906 for the same flight. Among the pilots were Wilbur Wright, the Comte de Lambert (one of Wright's early pupils) and Blériot, as well as Hubert Latham, a private owner who had recently acquired Antoinette No. IV. Latham was a popular and dashing pilot, whose championing and skilful demonstration of Antoinettes was largely responsible for their success.

Latham was the first to start, on July 19, and should have reached England easily. However, his normally reliable motor let him down and he had to be rescued in mid-Channel by an accompanying torpedo-boat.

Blériot, whose very much less reliable Anzani engine also nearly failed him, started on July 25 and at five in the morning skidded to a stop on the wet grass beside Dover castle, breaking his undercarriage in the process. In $36\frac{1}{2}$ minutes he had won the prize, assured the place of his monoplanes in the market and destroyed for ever the inviolability of England, hitherto protected by the Channel and her fleet.

Latham tried again on July 27 for the French prize, for which Blériot had omitted to enter in time, but once more came down in the water, a bare mile from the English cliffs.

Blériot searches for a low point to cross the English cliffs after his cross-Channel flight. An impression by John Young.

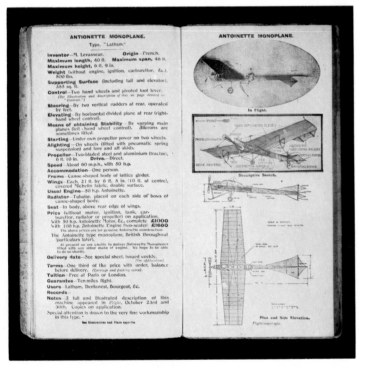

Above *The Antoinette (in this contemporary catalogue) cooled the water that absorbed the heat of the engine by evaporative means in the long copper tubes along the sides of the slender, graceful fuselage.*

Right *Latham, the unsuccessful Channel flyer, crossing the French coast. Like almost all photographs of this famous event, this is almost certainly a fake.*

Henry Farman flying his Voisin-Farman I-bis at Issy-les-Moulineaux, south of Paris, in the summer of 1908.

Early Biplanes in Europe

ONCE the French had recovered from the shock of the Wrights' demonstrations in 1908, which showed them how far they had slipped behind, they recovered rapidly. Indeed, with the Wrights now almost static in their design and Curtiss occupied with his first seaplanes, the initiative passed completely to Europe, with Germany and then Britain warmed into life by the French fire and inspired by the visits of the Wrights.

The place of Ferber in the development of the French biplane and his relation to the work of the Wrights has been described on pages 10 and 11. Ferber in his turn was to influence French thought profoundly. His stable, tailed aircraft reached right back to Cayley in basic theory. It was this, with the addition of the forward elevator introduced by the Wrights, that attracted the attention of Gabriel Voisin, who, with his younger brother Charles, set up the first aircraft factory in the world outside Paris.

Structurally based on the box kite invented by Hargrave in 1893, the Voisin became the definitive pusher biplane. The brothers built some thirty aircraft, including three gliders in 1905–1907, before the end of 1909.

Early in 1909, J. T. C. Moore-Brabazon, one of the first of the British sporting pioneers and a close friend of Charles Rolls, bought his second Voisin. Unknown to him, it had already been "sold" to Henry Farman and incorporated design features of his own. Following the inevitable row, Farman began designing his own biplanes, which became neater, better looking and more popular than the original Voisins.

Henry Farman and his aircraft were to become the best-known combination in the European flying world in 1910–1911. On November 9, 1907, with his original Voisin-Farman I, he made the first circular flight in Europe of 1 km. On January 13, 1908, he made another, this time officially observed, and on October 30 that year on the same machine, now much modified and with large ailerons fitted, he made the first genuine cross-country flight.

While this was going on in France, and the first British pilots were obtaining their brevets in France on French aircraft, a remarkable citizen of the United States, Samuel Franklin Cody, was preparing to make the first flight in Britain, which he achieved on October 16,

1908. Cody was a remarkable, flamboyant character, with the "honorary" rank of colonel. He designed and built his aircraft at Farnborough in Hampshire, England, home of the then Royal Aircraft Factory, and his huge biplane became "British Army Aeroplane No. 1." Better known as the "Cathedral," it had a wing span of 52 feet and weighed some 1800 lb. The engine, a 50-hp Antoinette, drove two pusher propellers with Wright-type chain drive.

As Cody did not become a British citizen for another year, the honor of being the first Englishman to fly was left to J. T. C. Moore-Brabazon (although his claim to the honor occasioned a dispute with another British flier, A. V. Roe, that was settled only after a committee appointed by the Royal Aero Club, under Lord Gorell, decided in his favor).

Above *Samuel Cody's third design, the 1911 Circuit of Britain biplane with a 60/80-hp Green motor, seen here at the Whitsun meeting at Hendon, England, in 1912.*

Left *The French sculptor-pilot, Léon Delagrange, on the Voisin-Delagrange I, built for him by the Voisin brothers in 1907. This was about as high off the ground as it ever got.*

One of many imitations—almost exact copies—of the very successful 1909 Farman, this Bristol Box-kite was an early British military trainer.

The Big Meetings

IF 1908 had been a year of tremendous development in aviation, with the emergence of Curtiss and others in the United States and numerous European pioneers, almost entirely from France, 1909 was a year of triumphant achievement. Symbolizing the great progress in the year since the Wrights came to France, the Rheims meeting, held between August 22 and 29, drew together the leading pilots and designers and presented a successful pageant of aviation. The distinguished international audience was headed by the President of the Republic, M. Faillières, and included Lloyd George, then British Chancellor of the Exchequer, as well as numbers of the military.

La Grande Semaine d'Aviation de la Champagne, to give it its proper title, financed and sponsored by the champagne industry and with the president as its patron, was the first event of its kind in the world. It exercised considerable influence on the later development of aviation, not only in technical matters (competition at the meeting was fierce) but by awakening in official minds some glimmer of belief in flying as a useful art. Unlike many of the thousands of meetings that were to follow down the years, it also made money.

Curtiss was at Rheims, with his biplane, and achieved the highest speed over a 30-km course with 46½ mph. Three Wright biplanes with French pilots completed the American presence. There were three Antoinettes and

four Blériots—two of the latter were of the cross-Channel type, the others were rather fussy elaborations of the Type XI. One of them, the Type XII, featured ailerons instead of wing warping and a powerful 60-hp ENV motor which pulled the clumsy two-seater along at up to 37 mph. The remaining monoplane at the meeting was Robert Esnault-Pelterie's REP 2-bis, a curious but effective aircraft with a 30-hp tractor motor designed by the same man. At the Rheims meeting it appeared with ailerons that were operated in unison as elevators—the first successful "elevons."

Among the biplanes, besides the Curtiss and the three Wrights, there were three Henry Farmans. Clean, fast and practical, they were among the most popular and successful of the European aircraft of the time. Farman himself, with a new 50-hp Gnôme rotary replacing the earlier Vivinus of the same power in his Farman III, carried off both the Grand Prix for distance and the Prix des Passagers, carrying two passengers for the latter. For the distance prize he covered 180 km in 3 hours 4 minutes 56½ seconds. He also came second to Latham's Antoinette VII in the altitude prize. Latham, flying his second cross-Channel machine with a new 60-hp Antoinette engine, reached just over 500 ft. No less than seven biplanes designed by Gabriel Voisin flew at Rheims.

The most significant aircraft at Rheims, however, in terms of the next twenty years' development, was the Bréguet I, with a 50-hp Renault engine, which is discussed in detail on page 26.

Eugene Ely taking off after landing on the USS
Pennsylvania, *thirteen miles out to sea, in*
January, 1911.

Early Hydroplanes

IN 1908 the US Navy was becoming interested, in principle, in the possibility of using airplanes with the fleet: there were naval observers at the Wright trials at Fort Myer, near Washington D.C., when the army bought its first aircraft. However, it was not until 1910, when practical aviation had become assured, that the navy actually made a move.

In the spring of 1910 Curtiss had conducted bombing experiments at Lake Keuka, dropping lengths of lead piping onto–or near–a battleship-shaped target. On November 4, Eugene Ely flew a Curtiss pusher landplane off a platform rigged over the forward 5-inch gun of the third-class cruiser USS *Birmingham* in Hampton Roads, VA. Two days before this an accident had robbed James McCurdy, who had worked with Curtiss in the Aerial Experimental Association, of the honor of achieving the first flight from a ship's deck–he had been making plans for a takeoff from an ocean liner.

On January 18, 1911, Ely took matters a stage further, landing on the armored cruiser USS *Pennsylvania* and later taking off again. However, the navy authorities were not really interested in landplanes: they turned to seaplanes which could, they hoped, operate from existing warships, being hoisted in and out on boat cranes without the need for flying decks.

As was to be expected, Curtiss became very much involved. On January 26, 1911, he became the first man to fly a seaplane off the water, and on February 17 he was hoisted on board the USS *Pennsylvania,* lowered into the water, took off and flew back to shore.

In May he supplied the navy with its first amphibian, the Curtiss Triad, and a landplane. These, together with a Wright, were the first three aircraft ordered. Powered by a 75-hp Curtiss V8 engine, the Triad was the first of a number of seaplanes, flying boats or amphibians ordered for the navy.

Curtiss developed the single-engined flying boat through to the F type, which was in constant production until 1918.

Working with Curtiss in 1914 was J. C. Porte, a former lieutenant in the British Royal Navy. When millionaire Rodman Wanamaker financed Curtiss' plans for a flying boat to attempt the London *Daily Mail* £10,000 prize for the first direct transatlantic flight, Porte helped design the *America*. With two 90-hp Curtiss OX engines, it was found to be underpowered, and a third engine was added above the wing. This resulted in the re-design of the hull to include big sponsons that increased the buoyancy—a feature that was to remain in flying-boat design for twenty years.

When the war started, Porte, who would have been one of the *America's* two pilots, returned to Britain, and at his instigation the Royal Navy ordered several similar aircraft. Later modified as a result of Porte's operational experience into the Curtiss H-4, they were the basis of a long series of very successful big patrol boats, employed until about 1924 by both the British and the American navies.

Bottom In spite of their complexity and apparent fragility, the steel-tube and wooden spar structures of early aircraft were robust and easily repaired. The British Naval Air Service had eleven of these Wights, with 200-hp Salmson radials.

Below Sopwith's Bat Boat, shown here in an improved amphibian form, was the first British flying boat. It had a 100-hp Green engine.

The Flying Displays

AFTER the first great meeting at Rheims, a second was held in July, 1910, which repeated the social success, if it did not equal the technical advances, of the first. Nevertheless, the year 1910 was important because it was marked by several significant changes.

The popularity of the new Farmans was assured—they were to develop into one of the main types with which France and Britain went to war. The famous cross-Channel Blériot was imitated throughout the world, and one of the designs that owed much to Blériot's influence emerged as the Nieuport, a trim, neatly cowled affair, with a fuselage, unlike the Blériot, completely enclosed. Its Darrocq engine gave 45 mph on 20 hp.

Robert Morane was to found a line of fast, clean monoplanes derived from the same pattern as the Nieuport. Nieuport himself was to achieve permanent fame with his later war machines, the nimble biplanes that helped to win control of the air in 1916.

Flying meetings did not only take place in France. There were two famous opening meetings in Britain: at Bournemouth and at Blackpool. Several prominent aviators—Cody among them—were deprived of their licenses by the Royal Aero Club for taking part in the latter meeting, which had not been sanctioned by the Club.

Five other British meetings took place; there were more than a score in Europe, and three in the United States, at Boston Harbor, Los Angeles and Belmont Park on Long Island.

Brindejonc des Moulinais at Hendon in 1913.
The aircraft is the tractor monoplane
Morane-Saulnier.

The last was the most important, rivaling the 1909 Rheims meet in its influence, with great public and official interest and many international competitors. In 1912 the first hydro-airplane meeting took place at Monaco, and following the second one in 1913 the French held, also at Monaco, the first of what was to become the greatest series of aircraft races of all time. The first race for the Schneider Trophy was won by France; the second, in 1914, by Britain—a surprise for the rest of the world, as little had been heard of British aviation progress outside its own shores. In the years to come, up to its final year, 1931, the trophy was to be won also by the United States and Italy. In those countries and in Britain it came to provide the opportunity to test very advanced aircraft and engines, and the know-ledge thus gained was to go far towards providing the basis for the fighters that fought the Second World War.

As far as displays were concerned, among the most active of all airfields was Hendon, a few miles north of London. Here Claude Grahame-White, the proprietor, with a keen eye to publicity, staged flying displays, races and aerobatics every weekend for fashionable and not-so-fashionable London, and thousands flocked out to the flying ground to see their favorite aviators.

At Hendon, in 1913, the earliest display of aerobatics in Europe was seen. Aerobatics had in fact, already been "invented" by Pegoud, a Frenchman, who also distinguished himself by making Europe's first parachute jump from an aircraft.

By 1912 the airplane was beginning to interest the military, and this all-metal Bréguet, with folding wings and rugged undercarriage, shows thought for military virtues.

Three Famous Biplanes

IN spite of the appearance of a number of clean, fast monoplanes, the biplane continued to gain headway during the period following the first introduction of aircraft in some numbers. Mention has already been made of the Bréguet I seen at Rheims, the first tractor biplane that was to set the style for all time.

Bréguet was one of the first to set up a production factory, at Douai, France, in 1909. His aircraft were remarkably modern looking and many, including the No. I, had three-bladed airscrews. In 1911 he produced an articulated three-blader.

The Bréguets were all metal and, after the first two, were mounted on sturdy tricycle undercarriages, with comparatively wide chord tires. It is not surprising that Bréguet received military orders quite early: the ultimate version, the Type 14 of 1916–1917, became the standard French day-bomber in the second half of the war, equipping nearly sixty squadrons, as well as the 9th and 96th Aero Squadrons of the US Army.

One of the first of the British pioneers was a young man named A. V. Roe. In 1908 he was struggling at the Brooklands race track outside London to achieve flight with his tractor triplanes. His claims to have made the first flight in England by an Englishman were disallowed by the 1928 Gorell Committee in favor of Moore-Brabazon, who had learned to fly in France (see page 19).

Roe, however, developed his designs successfully, and in 1912, at the Military Trials, entered his Type G, the first cabin biplane in the world. Powered by a 60-hp Green engine, it failed to win the contest (which was won by Cody's great windy beast). From the Type G, Roe developed the Avro 504, a simple, rugged, docile trainer that became one of the best-known aircraft of all time in Britain, just as the Curtis JN–4, the "Jenny," did in the United States.

One interesting piece of history is attached to the Type G. During the endurance test at the Military Trials the pilot, Wilfred Parke, performed a number of steep dives to break the tedium of the flight, and at one point spun off a turn. Although spins were known, they were a source of terror: no one had ever found out precisely what caused them, nor how to get out of them, although one man had accidentally done so. Parke, however, kept his head and worked out what is now the standard recovery technique, making a great contribution to the furtherance of flying by so doing.

Right A. V. Roe, best of the British pioneer constructors, designed simple tractor biplanes that looked right. This is the Type D Avro.

The Avro Type G, famous as the first cabin
biplane, flew a record 7 hours $31\frac{1}{2}$ minutes on
October 24, 1912.

J. W. Dunne began work in 1907 on a sharply swept-wing tail-less biplane, in search of the ultimate in stability. Far ahead of its time, the Dunne took time to develop, and early experiments with it in various forms were not very successful. However, by 1910, when he had come down from Scotland, where he had been working for the War Office in great secrecy, to Eastchurch on the Thames estuary, his No. 5 was flying well. In 1912, he had, in the Dunne No. 8, an aircraft that was able to fly from Eastchurch to Paris, powered by the 80-hp Gnôme rotary.

The Burgess Company of Marblehead, Mass., built two Dunnes under license in 1916; with these, which had a magnificent rearward field of fire, the US Navy's earliest gunnery experiments were made.

The Burgess Company, of Marblehead, Mass., sold this aircraft to the Canadian Aviation Corps in September, 1914. This painting, by R. W. Bradford, shows it in flight just before delivery in Canada. Sadly, it was then sent to England, and never flew again.

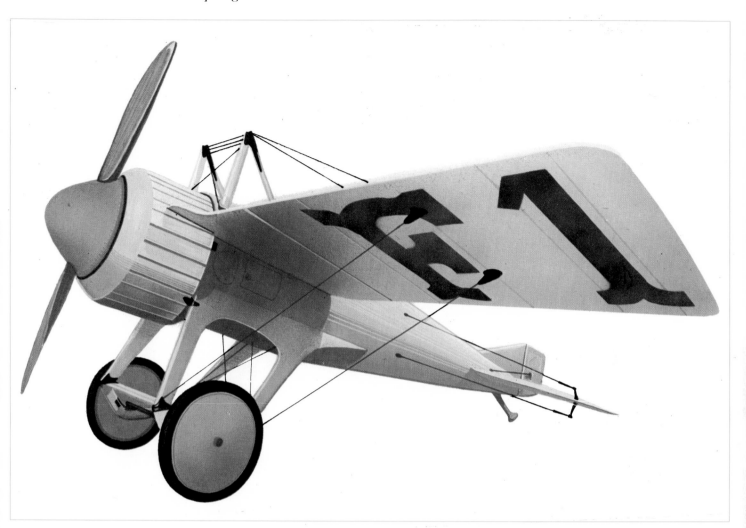

The beautiful Deperdussin racer of 1913 survives in a place of honor in the French Musée de l'Air. Illustration by Roger Gould.

A Look Ahead

AMONG the prophets of aviation there have always been, from time to time, men of vision whose designs or methods have outstripped those of their contemporaries. Unfortunately, in the early days of flying, their vision also outstripped the capabilities of construction and materials of the time, and thus their ideas had to wait for a later day to materialize.

When men were exploring every alley to advance the art of flight, some very curious theories were given solid shape. Sometimes, when they were the outcome of wrong thinking or expediency, they died, overtaken by new or simpler techniques. Sometimes they were simply attempts to get round the provisions of a too hastily granted patent application by a rival.

However, genuinely new ideas of great importance did appear, only to languish for lack of support. One such was the Deperdussin monocoque racer from France. Although at the time its complicated and expensive method of construction was against it, as its superior qualities were not yet needed, and the two-row motor had cooling problems, the firm went on to produce an armored, machine-gun armed military prototype and the Germans were to employ monocoque methods of building four years later.

Invented by a Swiss, the monocoque method of construction utilized the actual skin of the fuselage to take the aerodynamic loads imposed in flight, instead of using a wood or metal framework that could be covered with fabric or other material. With a few exceptions, the system was hardly used until the 1930s.

The Monobloc Antoinette was a serious attempt, in 1911, to reduce the drag of aircraft structures. This three-seater, although in fact it barely flew, featured a streamlined fuselage and an undercarriage enclosed by carefully profiled trousers. The most important aspect of its advanced design, though, was the fully cantilever wing—although not a success itself, it produced a crop of ideas for future designers.

Some American Pioneers

THOMAS Benoist was one of a number of men in Europe and the United States who turned from automobile manufacture to the airplane. With the money he had made from automobiles, he started an aircraft business at St. Louis in 1909.

That was the year that saw the great Rheims flying meeting, where the latest in flying machines showed their paces, and the results of the events and the records broken showed that the airplane was becoming at least half-way reliable.

Benoist, however, was a step ahead. He wanted to show that the airplane could be used, not just for sport or war, but for regular transportation. As a result, in December 1913 he signed a contract with the city of St. Petersburg, Florida, to provide a scheduled airline.

The St. Petersburg–Tampa Airboat Line started operations on January 1, 1914. Regular flights, two a day in each direction, were kept up, and when the contract terminated after three months the line had carried 1204 passengers, suffered only eight cancellations, and had paid its way. The line carried on a further month before ceasing operations at the end of the touring season – the first regular scheduled airline in the world.

Glenn Hammond Curtiss, the second of the American pioneers, and destined to as great a fame as the Wright brothers, cut his teeth as a designer and pilot with the Aerial Experiment Association, a joint Canadian-American venture based at Baddeck Bay, Nova Scotia and Hammondsport, Lake Keuka, in New York State, where Curtiss was later to set up his own base. Curtiss had a hand in the design and flying of the AEA's two gliders and four powered aircraft before he began his own operations.

Unlike the Wrights, Curtiss operated close to the great cities, and from the first was far more successful in achieving publicity. In 1910, Curtiss aircraft flew some notable cross-country trips, including one from Albany to New York City and a round trip between New York and Philadelphia, which inevitably made a great impression on the public mind.

His location on Lake Keuka encouraged his early interest in hydroplanes and flying boats, and the successful flights on and off warships (see pages 22–23) brought him into profitable contact with the navy, just beginning, in 1910–1911, to be interested in the airplane.

Another pioneer destined to leave his name among the famous aircraft builders was Glenn Martin. He began his career as a designer of powered aircraft in 1908, with a Curtiss-type pusher typical of the period. Like Curtiss he embarked on a series of public flights – later to be called "barn-storming" – to raise the funds to enable him to go on building, designing and flying.

In 1913 he made his first military contact, selling one of his designs, the Model TT, to the army. Later, he joined forces with the Wright Company to form Wright-Martin, but left them in 1917 to form his own firm. At one time, in the complex interplay of relations and mergers characteristic of the American aircraft industry, he was building a Curtiss torpedo-bomber, the CS of 1925, having underbid his rival for a production order.

31

The culmination of the early Avro biplanes came with the Type 504. It served for more than ten years as a military trainer and was universally used by British civil pilots in 1919–1920.

Military Beginnings

THE origins of the Avro 504 and the Farman biplanes have been explained. Although the Avro was primarily a training airplane, it began its military career in a far more aggressive manner, carrying out the first long-range strategic bombardment in history – with 20-lb bombs.

The Royal Naval Air Service had sent a force of aircraft to operate along the Belgian coast shortly after the outbreak of war, and they began a series of raids, principally against the German airship sheds established at Dusseldorf and Cologne. The Admiralty was entrusted with the defense of Britain against air attack, and the RNAS at Ostend were there to frustrate Zeppelin movements against England. Eventually they succeeded in destroying a Zeppelin, Z IX, in her shed at Dusseldorf, and a month later they mounted a bold attack on the very birthplace and source of the Zeppelin – Friedrichshafen on Lake Constance in southern Germany.

Right Maurice Farman's ponderous gentle pusher, the "Shorthorn," was an early example of Anglo-French standardization, being used extensively by both countries. Painting by Roger Gould.

Four naval Avro 504s, carrying four 20-lb bombs each, were positioned at Belfort in southeastern France, and on November 21, 1914, three of them set out for Friedrichshafen along the valley of the Rhine, studiously bending their course to avoid neutral Switzerland. They bombed successfully, damaging a new Zeppelin and destroying the gasworks.

This concept of striking at the source of the enemy's power was a remarkable anticipation of the whole future employment of air power, but it was not until 1918 that any serious attempt, and then on a small scale, was to be made to follow it up.

The big, slow, clumsy Farmans, like the Avro and all other aircraft of the period, began their career as "front line" types, until the gradual introduction of specialized reconnaissance and fighting aircraft enabled them to be relegated entirely to the training role.

Long reconnaissance against enemy rear areas in the cumbersome Farman Longhorns and Shorthorns were a feature of the first year of war, with more casualties from the unreliable Renault engines and the strong, unfavorable westerly winds than from enemy action itself.

Both the Longhorn and the Shorthorn were designed by Maurice Farman, Henry's brother, the names deriving from the forward elevator on long outriggers on the MF7 and its absence on the MF11. Pilots transferring from one to the other of these aircraft faced one of the earliest examples of the problem of coming to terms with a new type: apart from losing the psychological comfort of the big forward elevator, pilots on the Shorthorn, staring into the naked void ahead, had nothing to line up on the horizon for straight and level flying.

The first real step towards sensible training of pilots was made on the Avro 504, which equipped the Smith-Barry School of Special Flying at Gosport, England. At Gosport from 1916 onwards a graduated, standardized system of teaching flying was applied, for the first time anywhere in the world.

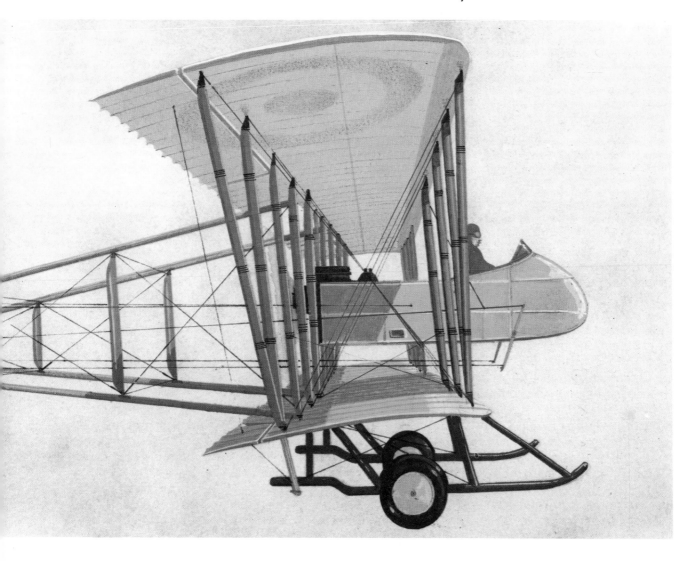

The Early Tasks

AIRCRAFT better suited to war than the Farmans were in existence in 1914. These were confined exclusively to reconnaissance work, partly because it had not seriously occurred to anybody, despite occasional experiments with machine guns before the war, that fighting in the air was possible. Initially, this was perfectly true. The difficulty of finding and pursuing another aircraft, where maneuvering was a cautious business and there were few aircraft in a vast sky, was reason enough.

The other and even more daunting reason was convincingly demonstrated in France when a German aircraft appeared over No. 5 Squadron, Royal Flying Corps' field one day in August, 1914. The squadron were feeling annoyed—one of their Avros had been shot down by the Germans that morning—and it happened that they had a Henry Farman armed with a private and quite unofficial Lewis gun, with which they gave chase. As the extra weight of the gun and gunner ruined

the already pitiful performance of the Farman, the gesture was futile.

The main reason for confining activity to reconnaissance, however, was that all three of the combatants in the West were convinced that this was the aircraft's only role, extending the range of cavalry scouting "over the hill." In this, both British and French were conspicuously successful. On that same momentous day, August 22, when 5 Squadron's crashed Avro gave the Germans their first information that the RFC were in France, and Sergeant Major Jillings of 2 Squadron was shot in the leg and became the first RFC casualty, the Corps scored a reconnaissance coup. In a series of twelve reconnaissance flights, it effectively spotted and reported the masses of von Kluck's II Army Corps at the start of their great encircling move around Paris. Two weeks later, on Saturday, September 4, Louis Bréguet and Lieutenant André Wateau, flying the former's own private aircraft, a Bréguet AG4, on a voluntary reconnaissance "pour la Patrie" across the

Left *From the early unarmed B-series two-seaters, like this Albatros B II captured by the British, came the fighting German C types, nearly as fast as contemporary scouts.*

Bottom *From Geoffrey de Havilland's BE, shown at the Military Trials of 1912, came the BE2c, a stable, stolid reconnaissance machine as useless for war purposes as could be imagined.*

Below *The early Bréguet military aircraft were conspicuous in their metal coverings—which earned them the nickname of "Coffee Pot." Though worthy types, they earned little praise.*

Marne, found von Kluck now wheeling south *short* of Paris. The information enabled Joffre, the French commander-in-chief, to halt the Germans in front of Paris in the historic battle of the Marne, and gained Bréguet a Croix de Guerre.

Part of the reason for the German southward movement was to trap the British Expeditionary Force, but von Kluck, though equally well served by his scouting pilots, failed to take advantage of their reports, and the BEF slipped away.

The German army had encouraged aviation from an early stage, facilitating the employment of military officers as pilots and observers, and creating, by means of competitions in 1911, 1912 and 1913, a number of good military scouting two-seaters with reliable water-cooled engines. These tough biplanes, with their 100-hp Benz or Mercedes motors, were available to cover the German army's fronts in 1914, and with constant development throughout the war they became difficult customers to tackle as air fighting developed.

The First of the Fighters

ALTHOUGH more or less private armaments began to be carried on two-seaters quite early in the war, proper air fighting, with aircraft designed for the task, did not begin for some months.

Many observers or pilots carried carbines or revolvers (the more optimistic took bricks along) and the French began to arm their big, load-carrying Voisins and Bréguets with Hotchkiss machine guns. On October 5, 1914, Sergeant Franz, of the *Armée de l'Air's* Squadron V24, with his observer-mechanic Quénault, shot down the first aircraft ever to be destroyed in air-to-air combat.

It was another Frenchman, Roland Garros, one of the pre-war pioneers, who started off the real shooting war. Before he was shot down by ground fire on April 19, 1915, Garros had destroyed five unsuspecting victims – unsuspecting because he had fired at them while approaching head on. Although this was the easiest way to shoot from an aircraft – aiming the gun with the aircraft itself – such an action should inevitably have smashed the propeller

Early success came to the French Moranes with the bullet deflectors for their airscrews. The system was used for some time in service with British and French aircraft, though it was a clumsy one at best.

36

of Garros' Morane. Somehow it did not.

He fell behind the German lines and was captured, and examination showed metal deflector plates on the rear of the blades, in line with the muzzle of the Hotchkiss.

Working in Germany at this time was a young Dutch aircraft designer, Anthony Fokker, who was busy supplying slim, 80-hp monoplane (*eindecker*) single-seaters to the German Army. Confronted with the Garros device, his factory came up with a practical interruptor gear for a forward-firing machine gun. Two weeks later the first armed Fokker Eindeckers arrived at the front.

There was no question of squadrons of these aircraft going into battle. The Fokkers, like all other deliveries at that time, reached the front one by one and were distributed singly among the units. The Germans, with tidier military minds, tended to group aircraft of the same type in one unit, but in general, squadrons of the British, French and German air forces were a mixture of different two-seaters, with odd single-seater scouts scattered among them.

Only in the summer of 1915 did Max Immelman, one of the two top German Fokker pilots, get the first three-ship fighting units formed with the Eindecker, and it was not until February, 1916, that the first RFC scout squadron entirely equipped with one type appeared on the front. This was No. 24 Squadron, with the DH2.

Through the summer of 1915 and into 1916 the handful of Fokker Eindeckers created havoc. Gradually the arrival of the pusher DH2 and the French Nieuport XI with a Lewis gun on the top wing (both planes thus getting over the Allies' lack of an interruptor gear) began to remove initiative from the Germans, and the arrival of the Sopwith Pup, derived from the 1914 Schneider Trophy winner, with a synchronized Vickers gun, marked the Allied revival.

Then, in August, 1916, the first of the new German Albatros scouts, the D I, appeared. It carried two machine guns, which gave it an enormous advantage (not only because of its double firepower, but because one gun frequently jammed), and its 160-hp Mercedes engine gave it a lively performance in spite of the extra weight. Back went the initiative to the Germans.

Typical of the huge German R-planes, five- or six-engined, was this Siemens-Schuckert R VIII (bottom), remarkably advanced in design despite its cumbersome appearance. The R VIII had six engines in the fuselage, driving four airscrews through long shafts. Although the big Sikorsky Ilya Mourometz bombers (below) may have been difficult to shoot down, they were, like their German counterparts, all too easy to wreck through control problems.

The Giants

THE big airplane, appropriately enough, came out of Imperial Russia. Igor Sikorsky, who had been concerned with early helicopter experiments and was later, in the United States, to produce the world's first practical rotary-wing aircraft, turned to conventional machines after building two helicopters in 1909 and 1910.

His first four-engined aircraft, the *Bolshoi*, with a span of 92 feet, 6 inches, made its initial flight on May 13, 1913, at St. Petersburg. A second aircraft, powered by 100-hp Mercedes engines, flew in January, 1914, carrying sixteen people to the *Bolshoi*'s eight. This was the Ilya Mourometz, which went into production at the Baltic Wagon Works as the world's first four-engined bomber. Enormous, stable, almost indestructible (only one was ever shot down), with special bombsights, the Ilyas of the special Flying Ship Squadron formed to operate them in 1915 did some damage to the Germans in the East. Both the French and the British were interested in building these giants, which continued operations right up to the Revolution in 1917, when they were destroyed by their crews.

Associated with Sikorsky in the design of the *Bolshoi* was an Englishman, C. J. H. Mackenzie-Kennedy, who had been designing aircraft in Russia since 1908. When Kennedy returned to Britain shortly after the war began, he started design and construction of his own giant aircraft. Giant indeed it was, spanning 142 feet and weighing almost ten tons, but it was badly underpowered with four 200-hp Salmson engines, and never flew. It was, nevertheless, a praiseworthy effort towards progress.

Among those, like Curtiss, who designed aircraft to attempt the London *Daily Mail* transatlantic prize was a German pilot, Hellmuth Hirth, who planned a six-engined seaplane.

Like Curtiss, he had to abandon his plans when the war started, but he too found a military use for the project. Taken up by Count Zeppelin, who had more experience than anyone in building large metal airframes, the flying boat became transformed into a series of giant multi-engined bombers at the Zeppelin-Staaken works. Other Riesenflugzeuge, or R-planes, were built by Siemens-Schuckert, Linke-Hoffmann, DFW, AEG and Dornier (also working for Zeppelin). Apart from the last named, R-planes saw service throughout the war on the Eastern front and in small numbers on raids against England. Altogether, around sixty of these remarkable

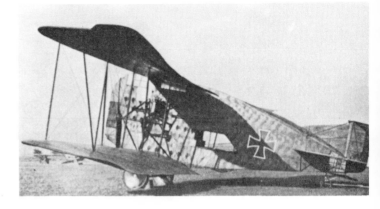

Another of the big R-planes, the Linke-Hoffmann R 1 40/16.

aircraft were built, about half of them seeing operational service.

They had wing spans of between 90 and 140 feet, were powered by four to six engines (some buried in the fuselage, driving airscrews through extension shafts), and represented huge steps forward in design and construction.

Being built on such an unwieldly scale, the planes suffered heavy losses from natural causes, but their designers and crews solved many of the problems of the next generation of aircraft: the last of the R-planes, the Zeppelin-Staaken E4/20 of 1920, was a very advanced civil airliner.

"For Valour"

"FOR VALOUR" is the motto on the Victoria Cross, the highest British decoration for bravery in the face of the enemy.

The three awards illustrated on these pages were all won in 1917, when the Royal Flying Corps faced a tough, aggressive and technically superior enemy, led by their new star, Baron Manfred von Richthofen. During one of many flights above the trenches, an FE2d, flown by Sergeant Mottershead of No. 20 Squadron, was set on fire at 9000 feet. While his observer sprayed him with a fire extinguisher, Mottershead brought the blazing aircraft down in a crash landing. The observer was thrown clear, but Mottershead, trapped in the wrecked plane, died of his injuries.

On March 20, 1917, Lieutenant Frank McNamara, of No. 67 (Australian) Squadron, landed his single-seat Martinsyde scout behind the Turkish lines to rescue a fellow pilot whose BE2c had force-landed. McNamara was already severely wounded in the leg, and the Martinsyde turned over when he tried to take off with both men aboard. Under heavy fire from Turkish cavalry they returned to the BE and succeeded in starting it, and McNamara flew the seventy miles back to his base.

None of the nineteen airmen who won the VC in the First World War deserved it more than Albert Ball. It was awarded him for his forty-three successful encounters with enemy aircraft between May 1916 and May 1917. He was the first of the British "air aces" at a very difficult time when casualties were particularly heavy, and his dashing attacks and determined fighting made him the inspiration of the entire RFC. Indeed, the two squadrons in which he served, Nos. 60 and 56, went on to become the highest-scoring and most-decorated squadrons of the corps.

Below *This painting by Stuart Reid shows the wounded McNamara escaping from the Turkish cavalry with Captain Rutherford.*

Bottom *A reconstruction by Norman Arnold of Albert Ball's last fight. In May 1917 Ball disappeared in his SE5 after a confused dogfight.*

The Gotha G IV and G V that raided England from the autumn of 1916 had a serious effect on British civilian morale.

The Night Bombers

IN spite of the initial success of the Zeppelin, it had proved an eventual failure when the British defenses obtained its measure, so the Germans turned to airplanes for long-range bombardment.

There were a number of twin-engined, long-range bombers in service on the Western Front in 1916, being used largely to develop techniques and systems. It was not until 1917 that the later versions of these began to be employed in the strategic offensive against England, and attacks on Paris and targets behind the front.

The 1917 Gotha G IV and G V had a range of some 300 miles—enough to enable them to reach London from their Flanders bases—and their two 260-hp Mercedes engines enabled them to bring their 650-lb bomb loads up the Thames estuary at 15,000 feet, far too high for the defense to reach them in time.

When the Gothas were caught, attacking machines faced a carefully designed defense that included a gun firing down through a tunnel to cover the standard blind spot beneath the tail.

The Zeppelin story was re-enacted with the Gothas. As the defense stiffened, the authorities withdrawing fighting squadrons from France in response to public outcry, the new British aircraft, the Bristol Fighter and the Sopwith Camel, cut unacceptably large slices from the Gotha force. In the autumn of 1917 they abandoned daylight bombing and after losing twenty-four aircraft shot down in twenty-two raids, finally stopped raiding altogether in May, 1918.

The British had not considered strategic bombing to any degree until the reaction set in against the Gotha raids, but when the Air Board decided to create a long-range bomber force there was already in existence the nucleus of an organization on which to work. This was the Royal Naval Air Service unit of Handley Page o/100 patrol bombers with which the RNAS had been night raiding happily throughout 1917. When united with the RFC's 41st Wing at Ochey, which flew its own Handley Pages, and squadrons of De Havilland single-engined day bombers, it formed the Independent Force, intended for strategic bombing.

As the war progressed, Sir Hugh Trenchard, head of the RFC, had seen more clearly that air operations required a separate force, controlling its own destiny and selecting its own missions. He was, however, loyal to his masters, the generals, and moreover most of his squadrons were firmly tied to army control. The creation of the Royal Air Force as a third service on April 1, 1918, gave him the opportunity he sought, and the Independant Force the means. Thickening up the night bomber offensive were numbers of the elderly FE2b. This big, Beardmore-engined two-seat pusher, with a superb field of fire for the front gunner, had survived since early combats with the Fokker monoplanes in 1916. (It was an FE pilot and gunner who shot down Immelman, the great Fokker ace.) Now they were working under cover of darkness, trundling their bomb loads to German airfields, railroad stations and ammunition dumps; it was these "Fees" that provided the expertise for the strategic bombers.

Top *When British retaliatory bombing started, it was with this naval Handley-Page o/100 type of 1917. It was the first big Allied night bomber of any performance.*

Above *Developed from the o/100, the Handley Page o/400 shows its neatly cowled Rolls-Royce engines, folded wings for hangar stowage, and the bombsight below the Lewis gun in the nose.*

PUBLIC WARNING

The public are advised to familiarise themselves with the appearance of British and German Airships and Aeroplanes, so that they may not be alarmed by British aircraft, and may take shelter if German aircraft appear. **Should hostile aircraft be seen,** take shelter **immediately** in the nearest available house, preferably in the basement, and remain there until the aircraft have left the vicinity : do not stand about in crowds **and do not touch unexploded bombs.**

In the event of **HOSTILE** aircraft being seen in country districts, the nearest Naval, Military or Police Authorities should, if possible, be advised immediately by Telephone of the TIME OF APPEARANCE, the DIRECTION OF FLIGHT, **and whether the aircraft is an Airship or an Aeroplane.**

GERMAN
AIRSHIPS

BRITISH
AIRSHIPS

Note specially the shape of the Airships and the position of the passenger cars

ZEPPELIN

SCHUTTE – LANZ

PARSEVAL

H.M.A. ASTRA TORRES

H.M.A. BETA

H.M.A. BTA

H.M.A. PARSEVAL

Note specially the sloped-back wings of the German Aeroplanes

AEROPLANES

AEROPLANES

STAHLTAUBE MONOPLANE

RUMPLER TAUBE MONOPLANE

AVIATIK BIPLANE

ALBATROSS BIPLANE

D.F.W. BIPLANE

BRISTOL BIPLANE

BRISTOL BIPLANE

AVRO BIPLANE

AVRO BIPLANE

SHORT BIPLANE

B.E. BIPLANE

SOPWITH TRACTOR BIPLANE

H. FARMAN BIPLANE

SOPWITH TRACTOR BIPLANE

LONDON
PRINTED UNDER THE AUTHORITY OF HIS MAJESTY'S STATIONERY OFFICE.
By SIR JOSEPH CAUSTON & SONS, LIMITED, 9, Eastcheap, E.C.

To be purchased, either directly or through any Bookseller, from WYMAN & SONS, LIMITED, 29, Breams Buildings, Fetter Lane, E.C., and 54, St. Mary Street, Cardiff ; or H.M. STATIONERY OFFICE (Scottish Branch), 23, Forth Street, Edinburgh ; or E. PONSONBY, LIMITED, 116, Grafton Street, Dublin : or from the Agencies in the British Colonies and Dependencies, The United States of America, the Continent of Europe and Abroad of T. FISHER UNWIN, London, W.C.

1915

PRICE TWOPENCE

The Shuttleworth Collection in England still operate this LVG C VI of 1918, a German two-seater of the First World War.

Another Shuttleworth aircraft is this Bristol F2b, the greatest two-seater fighter of the war and the last to survive.

This painting by G. H. Davis of a British Independent Force De Havilland squadron under attack typifies the big running battles of 1918.

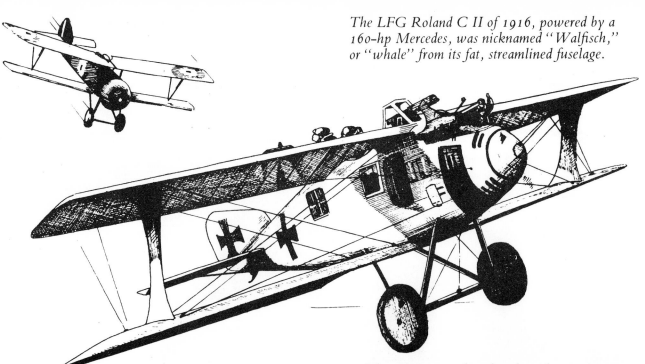

The Two-seater War

THE start of aerial fighting had seen the division of military aircraft into two quite clear classes–the reconnaissance plane and the fighter. The backbone of all air forces was the reconnaissance two-seater; its duty was to observe, map, photograph and report on the daily state of the war on the ground. With the introduction of the effective forward-firing machine gun came the possibility of interfering with enemy reconnoitering, and thus the start of air warfare.

Initially, these scouts operated singly, with roving commissions. It was not until problems of control and the escalation of the air war in 1916–1917 that fighting squadrons emerged. They forced the two-seaters to fight for their information, to carry guns and to work in formation for mutual protection.

Germany, with her air arm closely linked to her ground forces, developed her two-seaters into very efficient fighting machines, well suited to the tasks of army cooperation, contact patrolling and artillery work (controlling the shooting of the batteries) that were added to their original duties. Their powerful engines of up to 180–200 hp and sturdy construction made them difficult to catch or destroy and, unlike the British and to some extent the French, the Germans developed their designs steadily in response to new ideas and requirements. Some, like the Rumpler C IV of 1917, with a 260-hp Mercedes, were fast enough and flew high enough to evade Allied scouts on long, unescorted missions into rear areas.

The Germans also developed two interesting techniques with two-seaters. The availability of the LFG Roland C II, a fast, carefully streamlined aircraft, with one of the earliest wooden monocoque fuselages and good fields of fire for the observer, enabled them to operate big formations of the same aircraft type, of which some acted as escort fighters to protect the reconnaissance machines, with obvious advantages in control. The other innovation, which resulted in such aircraft as the Hannover CL II and III, was the production of specialized two-seaters for ground attack work–work with which the Allies, particularly the British, tended to burden their single-seater squadrons. The Hannover was small, having a span of 38 feet, and consequently agile. These qualities, plus very carefully designed fields of fire and the strong wood monocoque fuselage, made it extremely difficult to shoot down.

The British production of Corps two-seaters for army cooperation duties was largely in the hands of the government aircraft factory at Farnborough. Although this institution had produced some excellent prototype and experimental aircraft, its response to the demand for reconnaissance aircraft was woeful. Somewhere between the indifference of the high command and the conservatism of a government department, there emerged such unimaginative aircraft as the BE2c and RE8, stable, slow, outdated and almost totally incapable of showing fight or flight. In spite of large escorts of scouts in the latter half of the war, losses were high, rising to a peak during the two great periods of German domination of the battlefield, the "Fokker scourge" of 1916 and "Bloody April" of 1917.

Below *Evidence of the fighting qualities of the German two-seaters is given by this British diagram of recommended fighting methods.*

Bottom *These RE8 Corps two-seaters of 15 Squadron stand among a litter of empty fuel tins and stores in France.*

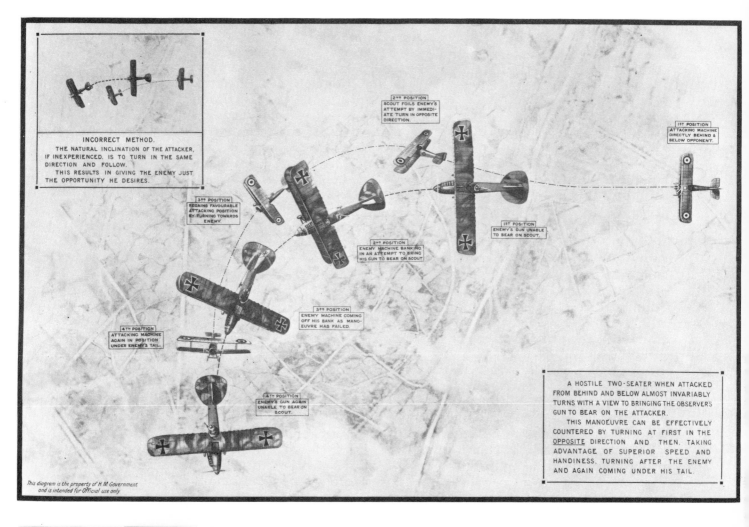

Best-known and most widely used of the French aircraft in the service of the American Expeditionary Force was the SPAD.

The Fighting Scouts

THE Allied fighters brought into service to combat the Fokker Eindecker in 1915 and early 1916 were what might be called interim types: the 100-hp DH2 pusher and the 80-hp French Nieuport 11 (first ordered by the RFC), each with a single Lewis. They were followed by the Nieuport 17 with a 110-hp Le Rhône rotary and the Sopwith Pup, with an 80-hp version of the same engine. Both were outstanding aircraft, light, very maneuverable and well able to deal with the opposition. A significant newcomer at this time was the French SPAD VII, with the big, heavy, 175-hp Hispano-Suiza engine, and a much stronger airframe than the Nieuport. It had one Vickers gun and a top speed of 119 mph, compared to the Pup's 115 mph and the Nieuport 17's 110 mph.

Then, in the autumn of 1916, the Germans introduced the Albatros D I and D II. Derived, like the Pup and the Nieuport, from a prewar racing aircraft, it had a 160-hp Mercedes engine that gave it a very fast climb and, although it was slower than the lighter Allied scouts, it carried two machine guns.

This 100-per-cent increase in offensive armament gave the Germans a great advantage. Against it the French, in April 1917, introduced a new SPAD, the S XIII, with a 235-hp Hispano and two Vickers guns. (By this time an improved Albatros, the D III, was ready.) The S XIII was one of the best aircraft of the war, built in large numbers (8472) and widely used by the AEF. It equipped, eventually, eighty-one French and sixteen American squadrons. Sopwith produced a 200-hp rotary-engined successor to the Pup, nicknamed the Camel, from the hump that concealed its twin Vickers guns. It was a devil to control, because of the gyroscopic forces of its heavy Bentley engine, but lethal in skilled hands. It scored 1259 victories, the largest tally for any single type. In parallel production was an admirable product of the Royal Aircraft Factory, the SE5a. Powered by the same

Hispano as the twin-gun SPAD, armed with Vickers and Lewis guns, it complemented the Camel, and a number went to see service with the AEF.

Although the earlier Allied pilots, like Albert Ball, the first British ace, were reluctant to exchange their handy little rotary scouts for the later types with their heavy stationary engines and stiffer handling, it was not long before the Allies had regained control of the air. German attempts to counter this were based on the new Albatros D V and Anthony Fokker's new triplane, the Dr I, with the 110-hp Oberursel rotary. Unfortunately, Albatros, or the German authorities, had failed to see the magnitude of the Allied gain and the D V offered little advance over earlier types. Moreover, both it and the low-powered triplane suffered a disastrous series of structural failures. It was not, in fact, until the arrival of the Fokker D VII, designed, like all Fokker's aircraft, by the brilliant Reinhold Platz, that Germany could once more put into her pilots' hands a war-winning weapon.

With the 185-hp BMW water-cooled in-line engine, the D VII had an outstanding performance, including 124 mph maximum speed and superlative flying qualities. Unfortunately for its employers, it arrived too late to affect the outcome of the war.

The Royal Aircraft Factory SE5a single-seater, with one Vickers and one Lewis gun, was powered by Hispano-Suiza. It became a deadly weapon in the hands of experienced pilots. Painting by Brian Withams.

Lively and fast-climbing, the Sopwith Triplane was the aircraft from which the Fokker was supposed to have been copied. This one, from Raymond Collishaw's famous "Black" flight, is engaged with an Albatros D V. Painting by R. W. Bradford.

The Sea Flyers

NAVAL aviation during the First World War has always been regarded rather as a side show. Certainly it was neglected, and much of its effectiveness went unnoticed by officials and public alike. Despite this, considerable progress was made in the development of the techniques of operating aircraft with the fleet.

Three basic aspects of naval air war, the torpedo, the catapult and the aircraft carrier, had all been brought to reality before the war started. The early US Navy flights from ships have been described; in Britain the first takeoff from a ship was made by Lieutenant Samson from HMS *Africa* with a Short S27 landplane. The flight took place on January 10, 1912, and on May 9, Lieutenant Gregory created history with the first takeoff from a moving ship at sea, flying another S27 from HSM *Hibernia*. On November 12 the same year, Lieutenant Ellyson of the USN made the first catapult launch in the Curtiss AH-3.

Only the Armistice stopped massive attacks by carrier-borne landplane torpedo bombers of the Royal Navy. A squadron of these Sopwith Cuckoos was on board HMS Argus *in October, 1918, carrying 1000-lb torpedoes.*

The Royal Navy did not like airplanes—they looked as though they might upset Britain's traditional supremacy in battleships, but since they were there, they made use of them. The first aircraft carrier was commissioned in 1913 (and sunk by a submarine in October 1914), and altogether the Admiralty commissioned ten seaplane carriers during 1913–1916.

The curious thing about this aspect of naval air warfare is that it took so long to develop the true aircraft carrier. Although most of the British ships had flying decks, they were rarely used and the largest, *Campania,* used hers only for launching seaplanes from wheeled trollies. At the end of the war two ships, *Furious* and *Argus,* had flying on and flying off decks, but in the minds of authority the two operations were still quite separate and in fact, the emphasis was always on the seaplane, launched overside and recovered by crane. Unfortunately very little was accomplished, as the seaplanes of the period were frail, unreliable and mostly both underpowered and overloaded. In spite of this the RNAS bombed ships, sought out submarines, spotted for their battleships' guns, tried out radio and even torpedoed two Turkish merchant ships in the Mediterranean. (The first successful torpedo drop from an aircraft had taken place on July 28, 1914.)

The most effective of the naval aircraft were the big flying boats. Developed, mostly by John Porte, from the prewar Curtiss *America,* the Felixstowe F2A and F3, with two 345-hp Rolls-Royce Eagle engines and four machine guns, were outstandingly successful. They patrolled the North Sea and Mediterranean, sank submarines and shot down Zeppelins and fought intense battles against the German seaplanes based in Flanders.

American participation in the sea-flying war was, naturally, not large. The US Navy possessed only 54 aircraft when it went to war, but had 2017 at the end. (There were 740 aircraft with the American Expeditionary Force (AEF) in France at that time, in 16 squadrons.) First to go to war as a complete unit, with antisubmarine patrols from the Azores, were (almost inevitably) the Marines, with their 1st Aeronautic Company.

Left The Curtiss H-12 Large America was one of the most successful patrol flying boats. This is No. 8681 of the Royal Naval Air Service.

Above *The first experience in France for US aviators was the training camp. This charming drawing by French artist Marcel Jeanjean contains all the elements of that bewildering stage of service.*

Left *Encouragement to join the Air Service. The anonymous aircraft bears the original star markings that, for service in France, were changed to roundels like those of the DH4s, to avoid confusion with German markings.*

Top right *The first experience of aircraft in war for the United States came with the Mexican Punitive Expedition of 1916. The Curtiss JN-4s could locate the elusive Pancho Villa— even if they once almost got caught by the crowd—but the army still had trouble catching him. An artist's impression.*

Right *Air supply had its early beginnings in 1915 when Voisins dropped supplies to beleaguered Kut-el-Amara. It became more practical on the Western Front in 1918, when water and ammunition were dropped to forward troops. Here AEF DH4s supply US troops cut off in the Argonne, October 6, 1918. An artist's impression.*

The all-metal Junkers CL1 or J10 two-seater battleplane, with a 180-hp Mercedes engine, appeared in mid-1918.

The Dividends

THE much-quoted belief that the technical progress of aviation was speeded up by the war has been questioned, with some justification. Leaving aside any question of military progress in the employment of aircraft, it does seem doubtful that anything came out of the "forcing house" of war that would not have been done better and just as quickly in peace-time, without the distractions and frustrations of wartime controls.

Technically, metallurgical and aerodynamic research had probably been speeded up. Engines were slightly more reliable, though scarcely more powerful. The average hp in 1913 had been between 80 and 160 and by 1918 had risen to 110–250. Really promising pre-war ideas, such as the variable-pitch propeller, had been smothered by the wartime necessity to concentrate on first things first. Other advanced ideas, such as the beautiful monocoque wooden fuselages of the German Albatros, Roland and Hannover aircraft, were still-born, partly because of the innate conservatism of the industry, and partly because of the great difficulty, for some years after the war, in financing expensive new techniques or subsequently justifying them by sales.

There were, of course, exceptions. Two notable aero engines went into production

during the war. The Rolls-Royce Eagle, giving 375-hp, was to power many record-breakers, and with its stable-companion, the 275-hp Falcon, was the foundation of perhaps the most famous line of aero engines in the world.

In the United States, the 400-hp Liberty engine, rushed into production to power the thousands of aircraft on order for the 1919 campaign, none of which were ever built, suffered heavily from teething troubles in its early days. But it, too, emerged as a very reliable engine that supported the aircraft industry for many years.

One of the most significant developments to emerge from the war, though not as a result of it, had a quiet beginning at Döberitz, near Berlin, on December 12, 1915, when Lieutenant von Mallinckrodt made the first flight of the Junkers J1. First of its kind in the world, this all-metal, cantilever monoplane was the start of the realization of one of Professor Hugo Junkers's dreams. Covered with sheet iron, because aluminum for such a dream was unobtainable in wartime, the "Tin Donkey" remained unique. But further designs followed, and in 1917 Junkers produced the J4, a cantilever, armored biplane, in response to the requirement for a ground-attack or trench-strafing aircraft. It was large, and very heavy, weighing a ton and a half—its crews called it the

"Furniture Van." But it was safe—with engine, fuel and crew protected by $\frac{1}{4}$-inch of armor.

The wings were built of multiple tubular spars with load-bearing, corrugated-metal covering, a process that was the basis of many Junkers designs. Two hundred and twenty-seven were built.

Taking his theories a stage further, Junkers produced two other military aircraft. These were completely metal (the J4 had a fabric-covered rear fuselage) and were skinned completely with corrugated duralumin. The single-seat J9, powered by a 185-hp BMW engine, appeared in March, 1918, and all forty-one built saw active service—the first all-metal warplane in service in the world. Deliveries of the J10 two-seater were just beginning at the end of the war.

Above *The Junkers J1 (or J4 in the factory designation) came to the Infantry Support Squadrons of the Imperial German Air Service in 1917.*

Below *The Hannover CL II was the first of a new two-seat fighter category introduced by the Germans in 1917—the equivalent of the Bristol Fighter.*

Frank Luke was one of the fastest-scoring pilots of the war. With the 27th Aero Squadron he destroyed fifteen balloons to win the Congressional Medal of Honor. (Captain Beauchamp-Proctor of the RAF, highest balloon scorer, shot down sixteen.) An artist's impression.

Frank Luke was one of the fastest-scoring pilots of the war. With the 27th Aero Squadron he destroyed fifteen balloons to win the Congressional Medal of Honor. (Captain Beauchamp-Proctor of the RAF, highest balloon scorer, shot down sixteen.) An artist's impression.

The Balloon Busters

AT first sight, it seems unlikely in the extreme that such an inoffensive looking object as a captive balloon should rouse the passions that it did. The balloons, however, which were a permanent feature of life on the Western Front throughout the war, housed observers whose days were spent noting activity in the trenches, locating hostile batteries and generally spying.

They were extremely unpopular, and they were very vulnerable, being filled with inflammable hydrogen gas. In consequence, they attracted the attention of enemy scout pilots, and they soon became heavily protected by concentrations of antiaircraft guns and a singularly nasty German pyrotechnic known as a "flaming onion." The majority of pilots on either side left balloons severely alone if they could; attacking them was a hazardous and uncertain sport. There were a small number, however, who regarded the balloon as a challenge and specialized in their destruction.

The greatest of these pilots was Frank Luke, an Arizona copper-mine worker, who joined the 27th Aero Squadron in July, 1918. Between August 16 and September 28 that year he scored twenty-one victories, fifteen of them balloons. Not only was this a high score for these hazardous targets, but it was also one of the fastest scores on record.

A French naval lieutenant, Y. P. G. le Prieur, invented a light rocket, which was carried on the interplane struts of various Allied aircraft, four or five a side, and electrically fired. These rockets were a more useful weapon against balloons than the Buckingham incendiary ammunition of the Vickers gun—if they could be accurately aimed, which was quite another matter. They were used on the little Nieuport scouts, on BE2cs and on Horace Farman F40s, among other aircraft.

Albert Ball, who numbered a balloon among his score, foreshadowed the methods of the Luftwaffe in the Second World War when, on occasion, he used le Prieur rockets to break up enemy aircraft formations before selecting his victim, thereby depriving them of mutual fire support. The essence of attacks upon balloons was speed and surprise. It was essential to reach the balloon either before the attacker was overwhelmed by the anti-aircraft barrage or defending aircraft, or before the balloon itself was winched down to the ground out of harm's way.

The observation balloon and the private war that grew up around it were unique to the First World War, although it was not the first employment of the balloon in war. The French had employed one at the Battle of Fleurus in 1794, and the British had sent balloons to South Africa in the Boer War.

Transition to Peace

WHEN the Great War ended, on November 11, 1918, all the combatant nations except one were in possession of vast inventories of aircraft. The exception was the United States, where the enormous program of construction had not yet begun to get under way. The Royal Air Force held over 22,000 aircraft on its books, the French 10,000 and the Germans 20,000.

Eventually, most of these would find their way to the scrap heap, for peacetime requirements were minute compared to those of the expanding war. Anyway, if the peace parties were to be believed, warfare had been banned effectively for ever. There was one task, however, in this area, that the Allies fell upon with peculiar relish: the total destruction of the German Air Force. The Treaty of Versailles, which laid down the conditions for peace, was explicit. Of the total German military air strength, which included 2400 bomber, fighter and reconnaissance aircraft in the front line, 15,000 were to be surrendered, with 27,000 engines. The treaty was signed in June 1919, and in January 1920 the Allied Control Commission was charged with implementing it.

One of the great adventures in aviation after the First World War was the first trans-Canada mail flight. This painting by R. W. Bradford shows the final triumphant section across the Rockies from Calgary to Vancouver flown by Captain G. A. Thompson in a DH9A.

These ex-military trainers, Avro 504Ks (see p. 32), converted into three-seat seaplanes, gave joy rides along the British coasts after the war.

A sinister game of hide and seek developed, with the Germans trying to hide such stocks as they needed and to conceal the activities of their aircraft firms. The Control Commission officers, knowing or suspecting what was going on – and perhaps unconsciously implementing the famous promise to squeeze Germany "till the pips squeak," destroyed everything they found, including some promising civil projects.

One of the most advanced aircraft of its time, the Zeppelin-Staaken E4/20, fell victim, quite unjustly, to this zeal. It was a four-engined civil airliner, the design of which stemmed from the wartime R-planes. It differed, however, in being a cantilever monoplane, all metal, constructed principally from duralumin. There had been similar bomber projects on hand at the end of the war, but the E4/20 was intended for a commercial service between Friedrichshafen, home of the Zeppelin Company, and Berlin. After a number of successful flights in

1920, the commission insisted on its destruction, and it was scrapped in 1922. It would be a decade before anything comparable appeared on the world's air routes.

An equally advanced aircraft that did survive the treaty was the Junkers F13. A civil airliner, seating four passengers, it was developed from the J10 and flew in 1919. Strong and reliable, it became the first airliner to achieve international sales. Production, spread over thirteen years, totalled 322 – a very large number, when most airliners were only built in dozens at the most.

While every manufacturing country was developing civil aircraft from wartime designs, at the other end of the scale ex-war pilots were making a precarious living giving flights in surplus military trainers. The barnstormers in the United States with their Curtiss Jennies, and the joyriders in Britain with their Avro 504s were a large part of the aviation scene in the postwar years.

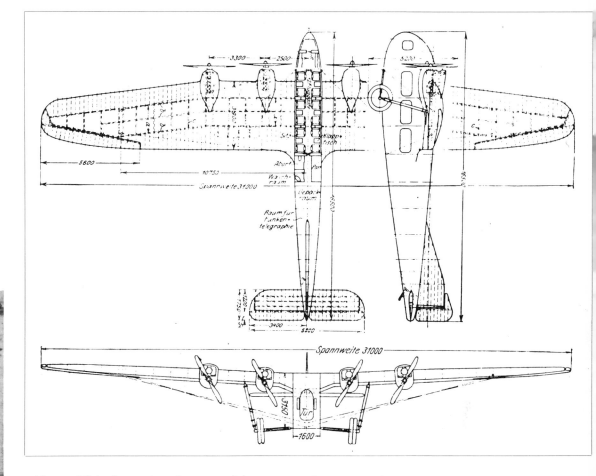

Above *This three-view drawing of the Zeppelin Staaken E4/20 shows clearly the advanced design thinking that went into it. Sadly, it flew little before being scrapped.*

Below *From the advanced metal Junkers battleplanes came this F13, the first internationally successful airliner – seen here in Germany with skis for winter operation.*

The first crossing of the Atlantic—though not non-stop—was the achievement of this big US Navy Curtiss NC-4 flying boat. It was designed to operate from the open sea, and the high tail was meant to keep controls clear of the waves. Painting by John Young.

The Explorers

THE war had made everybody very much more conscious of the world they lived in, as faraway campaigns and naval battles brought the corners of the earth closer to home. Afterwards, the more daring set out to explore the world—by air.

The British went off to link their scattered empire with aircraft. Two Australian brothers, Ross and Keith Smith, flew home in a Vickers Vimy bomber, powered by two Rolls-Royce Eagle engines, leaving Hounslow, one of the London airfields, on November 12, 1919, and reaching Darwin, Australia, on December 10 to win the £10,000 prize offered by the Australian government. Quintin Brand and Pierre van Ryneveld struggled to the Cape, having crashed and written off their original aircraft—another Vimy—on the way. In the United States, both army and civilian pilots were busy spanning their great continent. An army crew flew right around the country in 1919, while the first transcontinental flight took place in 1921. Jimmy Doolittle, then a lieutenant in the Army Air Service, made the first coast-to-coast crossing inside twenty-four hours in 1922 in a DH4B.

The great prize, though, was the Atlantic. This best-known and most traveled ocean had been the goal of pioneer airmen ever since Walter Wellman set off in his airship *America* from Atlantic City on October 15, 1910, but was forced down 375 miles east of Cape Hatteras. The *Daily Mail* prize of 1913 was still to be won, and a number of crews assembled in Newfoundland in 1919— or destroyed their hopes in accidents en route. The first direct crossing was eventually made on June 14–15, 1919, by John Alcock and Arthur Whitten-Brown, almost inevitably in a Vickers Vimy, crash landing in western Ireland. Before this, however, between May 16 and 31, a US Navy flying boat, the Curtiss

Below *What the Avros were to Britain, the "Jennies" (JN-4s) were to the United States in the early 'twenties – trainers, barnstormers, doing everything and going everywhere. Painting by John Young.*

NC-4, had flown in stages from Trepassey Bay, Newfoundland, to Plymouth, England, via the Azores and Lisbon.

The NC-4 was one of a series of Naval Aircraft Factory boats designed for U-boat hunting during the war and capable of (and intended for) delivery across the Atlantic by air to the Royal Naval Air Service. Three boats, NC-1, NC-3 and NC-4, were prepared for the postwar crossing; under the command of Commander John Towers they set out for the Azores. NC-1, with Commander P.N.L. Bellinger and NC-3, with Commander Towers, both landed in the open Atlantic. NC-1 sank, but Towers taxied 200 miles to the Azores, which NC-4, with Lieutenant Commander A. C. Read, had already reached. NC-4 continued alone on May 27 and reached England on May 31.

Five years later, a combined effort by the US Army Air Service and the US Navy sent a team of four Douglas World Cruisers – two-seat single-engined biplanes – around the world. Powered, like the Curtiss boats, by the 400-hp Liberty, one aircraft, *Seattle*, crashed in Alaska. Another, *Boston*, came down in the sea off Iceland and sank. The remaining aircraft, *New Orleans* and *Chicago*, completed the first around-the-world flight in history, covering 26,345 miles in 175 days, between March 17 and September 28, 1924.

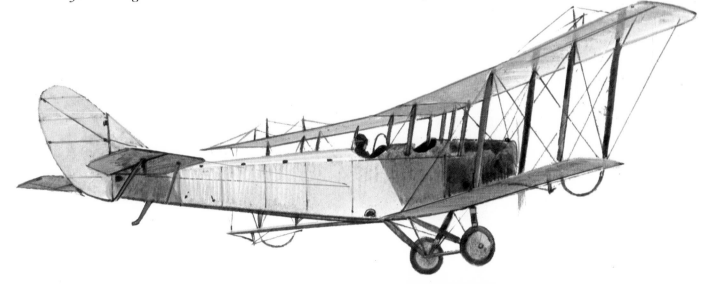

Commercial Dawn

THE success of the Vickers Vimy in long-distance record flying encouraged its designers to market a civil conversion for the airline companies that were beginning operations in Britain. Most of the routes were short, London–Paris being the most attractive, with others to various British and European cities. For reasons of economy and availability, single-engined converted De Havilland DH4s were frequently used.

The Vickers Vimy commercial, which featured a completely new fuselage, appeared in 1920 in the colors of Instone and Co., a shipping organization that, prophetically, was trying to get into the air travel business.

Handley Page had converted their o/400 bomber for civil work, and started their own airline from Cricklewood, their north London airfield, to Le Bourget at Paris. In 1921 they produced the first of a series of genuine commercial airliners based on the same design.

All British airlines ceased operation for a time in 1921 until a government subsidy, essential for competition with subsidized foreign airlines, was granted. A partial rationalization

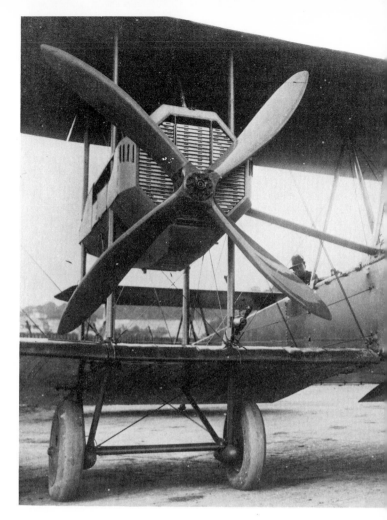

Above *Too late for the war, the Vickers Vimy bomber carried British pioneers to Australia and on the first direct Atlantic crossing.*

Below *The success of the Vimy encouraged Vickers to market a commercial version with airliner fuselage—but the venture, in 1920, was ahead of its time.*

of routes was organized to cut out wasteful competition, and the companies struggled on until 1924 when a government-owned national airline, Imperial Airways, was formed from the major companies.

The United States was spared this initial period of economic struggle with converted bombers. It was not until 1925 that the necessary legislation was passed to enable an airline to operate at all, and the development of airlines was based on the award of lucrative airmail contracts.

So essential were these mail contracts that most airlines almost totally ignored passenger carrying, regarding anything but an uncomplaining mailbag as a nuisance.

One outstanding exception to this philosophy was William Boeing. In 1928 he built passenger seats into his Boeing 40 Mailplanes, and these efficient aircraft enabled his bid for the vital and lucrative western section of the transcontinental mail route to undercut his rivals.

At this period, and up to about 1932, the major airlines were controlled by aircraft manufacturers, who built equipment to suit the route.

Right *The interior of the Vimy Commercial shows wicker chairs, pictures on the wall and large windows. On the bulkhead behind the cockpit are a clock, altimeter and speaking tube.*

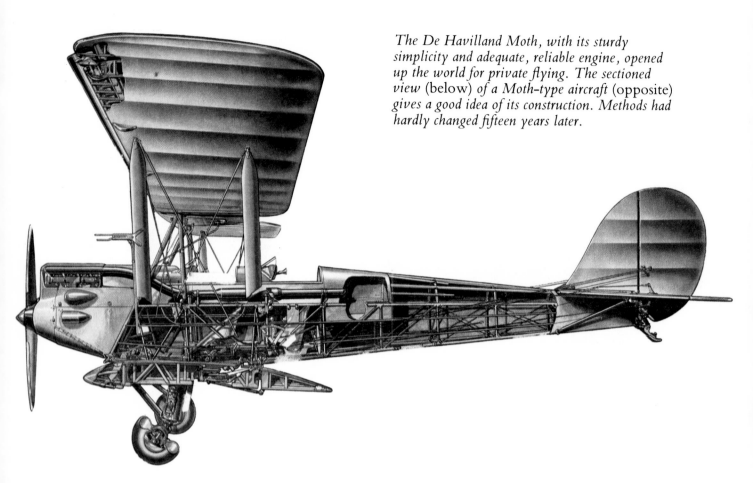

The De Havilland Moth, with its sturdy simplicity and adequate, reliable engine, opened up the world for private flying. The sectioned view (below) of a Moth-type aircraft (opposite) gives a good idea of its construction. Methods had hardly changed fifteen years later.

The First Light Aircraft

ALTHOUGH civil flying started up all over the world in 1919–1920, there was such a surplus of wartime aircraft being sold for virtually nothing that no market existed for a new aircraft for private owners and instruction. Nor was there a suitable engine for such a machine.

As various firms began to look for markets in the private sector, they had to make use of existing power plants, and in the United States the majority of often short-lived new designs came attached to the familiar Curtiss OX-5 or Hispano-Suiza engine.

In Britain, the Air Ministry sponsored competitions in 1923 and 1924 for new light-aircraft designs. Unfortunately, the emphasis was entirely on economy and low power and, particularly as the available motors were not at all reliable, none of the aircraft was remotely practical.

One man, Captain Geoffrey de Havilland, was encouraged to do something about this. As a young designer at Farnborough before the war he had been responsible for the BE2, a simple, robust and stable aircraft with im-

peccable manners, although none of these qualities saved it from being a disaster as a warplane. He had gone on to design the Aircraft Manufacturing Company's bombers and scouts during the war, starting with the DH2 of 1915. Since the war, under his own name, he had been turning out various civil airliners.

Now he turned to the ideal club and private owner aircraft, scaling down a larger design, the DH51. To provide the engine his friend Major Halford of the Aircraft Disposal Company designed a neat little four-cylinder in-line motor that was simply one bank of cylinders from the company's Airdisco V8. The Aircraft Disposal Company existed to dispose of the vast stock of surplus RAF material; their V8 engine was simply a refurbished Renault.

The new engine, called the Cirrus, gave 60 hp for a weight of 290 lb. The whole aircraft, now named the Moth, comfortable, easy to fly and strong enough for instruction, weighed 1300–1500 lb and had a top speed of 91 mph. Its success was immediate and the De Havilland Company dominated the new sporting flying market it had just created. Imitators were numerous, but none enjoyed the same success.

Below *This version of the Moth, one of the most popular, had a 60-hp Cirrus engine. Later models, with the D.H. Gipsy motor, were given double that power.*

This clipped-wing Nieuport-Delage biplane raced in the 1922 Coupe Deutsche, and the type held both speed and altitude records.

Fast and Safe

THE year 1919 saw the resumption of the great tests of speed that had been such a feature of prewar flying, and in the next two or three years all the great races were re-established and new ones added.

In France, the Gordon Bennett and Deutsche de la Meurthe races were revived, and a series of powerful racers, some specially designed, like the Nieuport-Delage monoplane, some versions of existing fighters like the Nieuport 29 and the SPAD-Herbemont, all powered by the 300-hp Hispano, fought out the honors.

Their pilots, men like Bernard de Romanet, a war pilot with eighteen victories, who was killed in 1921 on a De Monge racer, Sadi Lecointe and Jean Casale, another ex-fighter pilot, were the heroes of France.

Aside from the races, a Homeric battle for the world speed record began among these three. The first post-war record was set up by Lecointe on February 7, 1920, at a speed of 275.264 km per hour. Casale broke it the next day, de Romanet on October 9, and Lecointe retrieved it on the Nieuport-Delage a day later at 296.694 km per hour. On October 20, Lecointe raised the record to 302.529 km per hour, had this beaten by de Romanet on the SPAD-Herbemont, took it again twice, the second time at 341.023 km per hour, only to lose it, on October 13, 1922, to General Billy Mitchell, flying a 375-hp Curtiss Racer at Detroit at 358.836 km per hour. Lecointe regained the record four months later, after which, for the rest of the year, it changed hands three times among the US Navy pilots of the Curtiss Schneider Trophy racers. A year after

Al Williams had raised it to 429.025 km per hour, another Frenchman, Adjutant Bonnet, brought it back to France, to lose it to another Schneider Trophy pilot, this time an Italian. British or Italian Schneider pilots kept the records until 1939. At the end of our period, in September 1929, it stood at 575.7 km per hour, set up by a British Supermarine S6.

At the Gordon-Bennett 1920 race at Etampes, a futuristic American monoplane, the Dayton-Wright, appeared among the highly tuned but conventional biplanes. Behind the Hall-Scott 250-hp in-line engine the pilot sat completely enclosed in the deep, narrow fuselage, with no forward view at all, except through the side windows of his cabin. The wing, of hollowed balsa with ply covering, featured camber-changing front and rear flaps, and the undercarriage retracted into the fuselage (the first practical example).

This radically designed airplane, with features ten years ahead of its time, did not finish the race, thanks to a broken control cable.

One of the most remarkable international contests was the 1927 Safe Aircraft Competition sponsored by the Daniel Guggenheim Fund for the Promotion of Aeronautics. Designed to promote methods of improving the safety of flight, the rules specified a minimum level speed of no more than 35 mph, the ability to land in 100 feet from an approach speed of not more than 38 mph; and for takeoff, to clear a 35-foot obstacle 500 feet from the start, in 300 feet.

Only two aircraft, the Curtiss Tanager and the British Handley Page Gugnunc, qualified after all the tests, and the Tanager finally won the $100,000 first prize.

Winner of the Guggenheim Safe Aircraft
Competition in 1929 was the odd-looking
Curtiss Tanager (below), incorporating flaps,
leading-edge slots and floating ailerons.
Illustrated (bottom) is the runner-up, the
Handley Page Gugnunc.

From France came the Bréguet-Bidon, a very long-range record breaker. Painting by John Young.

The Atlantic Pioneers

THE North Atlantic had been crossed three times in 1919. Commander Read's NC4 had done it only in two stages, the Vimy of Alcock and Brown had got only as far as the west coast of Ireland. The third, double, crossing had been made by the British airship R34, in July. She took 108 hours to make the westward trip, and with an airship's ability to stay airborne, hardly comes into our story. In October, 1924, the German reparations Zeppelin LZ126, later the US Navy's ZR3 *Los Angeles,* also crossed to Lakehurst, New Jersey, without causing much comment.

There was still a feeling that the great crossing was yet to come. And three years later it did.

In 1919, Raymond Orteig, an American of French descent, offered a prize for the first direct flight between New York and Paris in either direction. For many years there were no takers, but by 1926–1927, with the lure of $25,000 in prize money and aircraft with the necessary performance just within reach, quite a number of competitors appeared. A series of disasters focused attention on what seemed to

be a most unlucky prize. René Fonck, a famous French wartime ace, crashed taking off from New York in 1926. Two other Frenchman, Nungesser and Coli, equally well-known, set off from Paris on May 8, 1927, with considerable publicity – and vanished. Just before this two Americans, Wooster and Davis, on a big trimotor Keystone, crashed and were killed in a spectacular takeoff disaster.

And then, suddenly, without fuss, on May 20–21, 1927, Charles A. Lindbergh had done it. Not only that, he had done it alone. This quiet, almost unknown airmail pilot had left Long Island in his tiny, single-engined Ryan monoplane, flying an economic and accurate Great Circle route, and landed at le Bourget to scenes of hysterical welcome, $33\frac{1}{2}$ hours later.

It is difficult, in an age when universal television and press coverage have robbed us of all surprise, to realize the impact of this gallant and stupendous achievement. Overnight the young, lone flier became an international hero. To this day, few people remember the two aircraft and the two airships that crossed before him, and the climax of his achievement, quite rightly, was that he had succeeded alone.

Two other aircraft achieved fame during this period of great flights around the globe. Louis Bréguet, in France, shortly after the war, had developed out of his wartime Br XIV a

long-distance bomber, the Type XIX, which
had been used for a number of records. It
was modified for these flights as the Type
XIX GR (for "Grand Raid," as the French
called long distance flights), and a final version,
the Type XIX TR Super Bidon, or "flying
petrol tank," capable of lifting over 860
gallons of fuel, regained for France the long-
distance record in 1929. In 1930, flown by
Costes and Bellonte, it made the first direct
Paris–New York flight – Lindbergh in reverse.

There was also an American aircraft designed by Guiseppe Bellanca as a testbed for
the new Wright J-5 Whirlwind motor in
1926. Its aerofoil section fuselage and wide,
lifting wing struts helped to give it an exceptional range, and in 1927 it set an endurance
record of over fifty-one hours without refuel-
ing. A month after Lindbergh this airplane
flew the Atlantic, and Bellancas went on to
make other long-distance flights.

*Below Guiseppe Bellanca produced several
variations of his big, load-carrying monoplanes.
Earlier versions of this Model F held many
distance and endurance records.*

In Germany, designer Claude Dornier's first commercial success came with the "Wal" or "Whale." This is a British-registered example.

Commercial Successes

ANOTHER record-breaking aircraft of the latter half of our period was the twin-engined German Dornier Wal. Dr. Claudius Dornier was one of the German pioneer designers and, like Junkers, had interested himself early in metal construction. During the First World War, working for Count Zeppelin, he produced a variety of designs, ranging from a tiny, 25-foot-span all-metal cantilever biplane scout (which featured a drop tank under the fuselage) to a series of giant multi-engined flying boats, none of which saw real service.

After the war, he continued his research into metal aircraft and combined it with his interest in flying boats, starting a factory at Altenrhein in Switzerland to overcome the ban on construction imposed by the Allies.

The Wal became the definitive Dornier flying boat, with a large, flat wing carrying the engines in tandem above it, and big sponsons to steady the long, graceful hull and provide extra buoyancy. It gave birth to the four-engined Super-Wal and later the carefully streamlined Do18 and Do26.

Wals were widely sold and undertook record flights on the Atlantic and into the Arctic, but their chief claim to fame lay in the part they played in the development of regular ocean crossings. (It was a German who had made the first east-west Atlantic airplane crossing in 1928 in a Junkers W33 – developed from the F13.)

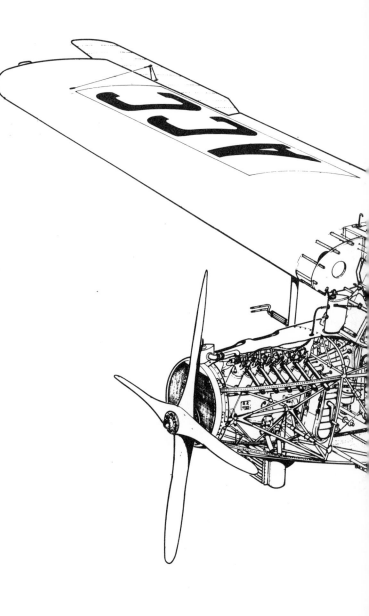

About the same time that the Junkers F13 was making its mark, Anthony Fokker, who had returned to his native Holland after his wartime services to Germany, and was now concentrating on commercial aircraft, introduced the Fokker F II, which made the first flight from the Netherlands to Britain in 1920. This was the prototype of one of the most successful series of airliners of the period, developing into the single-engined F VII and then into the famous F VII/3m. Like the Junkers, these aircraft had the distinction of achieving the first international sales, and the big Fokkers served with numerous airlines all over the world besides their native KLM.

They incorporated two of the design features that had made the firm famous, the thick-section, high-lift wing designed by Platz for the wartime fighters, and the welded steel tube system of fuselage construction that was almost a Fokker monopoly.

Fokker took an F II development, the F III, to the USA in 1921, but he was four years too soon for the commercial market there. Nevertheless, his construction methods aroused interest, and soon Boeing and Curtiss were using welded steel tube in their new fighters. Later, Fokker produced commercial and military aircraft in the United States.

MacReady and Kelly's transcontinental record in a single-engined Fokker T2 in 1923 foreshadowed a series of epic flights with the big trimotors. Kingsford-Smith in Australia and Richard E. Byrd in the United States, as well as a host of others, used the F VII/3m for transatlantic, transpacific and Polar flights, and an all-metal aircraft based on it, the Ford 5AT, was a highly successful airliner.

This cutaway drawing of the single-engined Fokker F VII gives an excellent idea of the constructional methods of Anthony Fokker and Reinhold Platz.

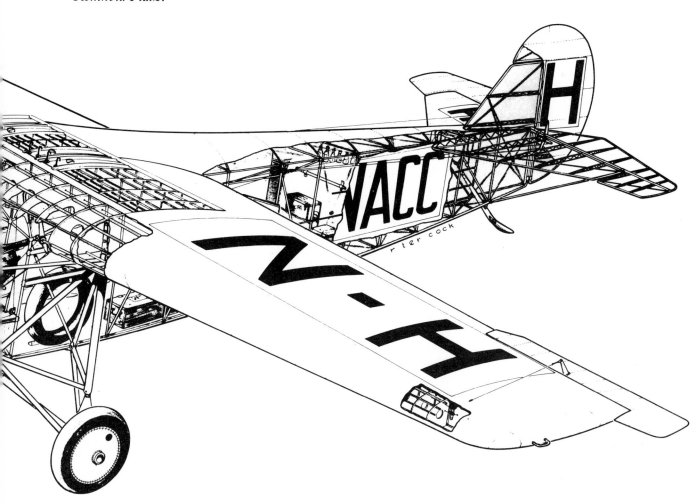

Power to Fly

IN no field of aeronautical endeavor did the United States rise so quickly to prominence as that of aircraft engines. Both the Wright and Curtiss companies, deadly rivals from the start in aircraft design, had been constructing engines of their own invention, though the two firms were eventually to merge their efforts in this field. The influence of the Wright brothers, incidentally, although remote as a direct result of their aircraft designs, was considerable during the formative period of the US aviation industry.

The original Wright company had been formed in 1909, and between 1910 and 1915 it delivered thirteen aircraft to the army's signal corps (out of a total army strength of fifty-nine machines).

In 1916 the company, with the Simplex Automobile Company, merged with Glenn L. Martin's Los Angeles firm to become Wright-Martin, building aero-engines for the US Government. About the same time the Dayton-Wright Company was organized to build aero-engines.

Martin left in 1917 to form his own company in Cleveland, Ohio. From the old Martin-Wright organization came the Wright Aeronautical Corporation (later part of Curtiss-Wright). Dr. Orville Wright became consultant to Dayton-Wright, and when that company was taken over by General Motors in 1923, many of the personnel formed their own organization, Consolidated Aircraft Corporation. All the early Wright engines were in-line, water-cooled designs (the company was the US licensee for the famous Hispano-Suiza), but the Wright designers built their first radial in the early 'twenties and then became identified with this type.

In 1925 the tool-making company of Pratt and Whitney, assisted by an ex-Wright engineer, began making radial engines. Later they were to combine with Bill Boeing's aircraft company and Hamilton Propellers to become United Aircraft. Boeing's first fighter, the PW-9 army pursuit plane, had a Curtiss D-12 engine, but when they were able to design around the radial Pratt and Whitney they began the famous line of navy biplane fighters, reaching 190 mph in 1929 with the P-12.

The Bristol Bulldog, with a neatly faired Bristol
Jupiter or Mercury radial of 450–480 hp,
served in several air forces.

Curtiss themselves were designing army
pursuits, with the experience gained in production of the D-12-engined racing seaplanes
for the Schneider Trophy. Their own 1929
design, the P-6E, achieved 192 mph. There-
after, in pursuance of a military decision to use
radial engines because of their lower weight,
simplicity and reliability, the liquid-cooled
vee engine dropped out of favor with American designers.

Its cause was not dead, however, as Curtiss
discovered. Glenn Curtiss was the first man to
market aero engines in the United States. The
Kirkham-designed OX-5 that powered the
Curtiss Jenny brought the company fame, and
the D-12, developing 450/480 hp, gave the
navy Curtiss racers many successes in com-
petitive events.

In 1923, Richard Fairey, a British aircraft
manufacturer, saw the D-12 and acquired a
license for it. Around it he built the Fairey
Fox, a two-seat bomber of such clean lines and
careful design that it outpaced the Royal Air
Force's fastest fighters and caused a sensation.
The close-fitting, low-drag cowling round the
D-12 gave the impetus to Hawker designer
Sidney Camm for a series of fast fighters and
bombers based on the similar Rolls-Royce
Kestrel engine.

*Curtiss's splendid D-12 in-line motor powered many famous aircraft, including this Curtiss CR-3
Schneider Trophy racer.*

Dr. Hugo Junkers, pioneer of metal construction and giant aircraft, dreamed of a flying wing and designed this J 1000 project (bottom) as far back as 1921 to carry 100 passengers in the 262-foot-span wing. Though the J1000 was never built, Junkers came halfway towards his dream with the G38 (below).

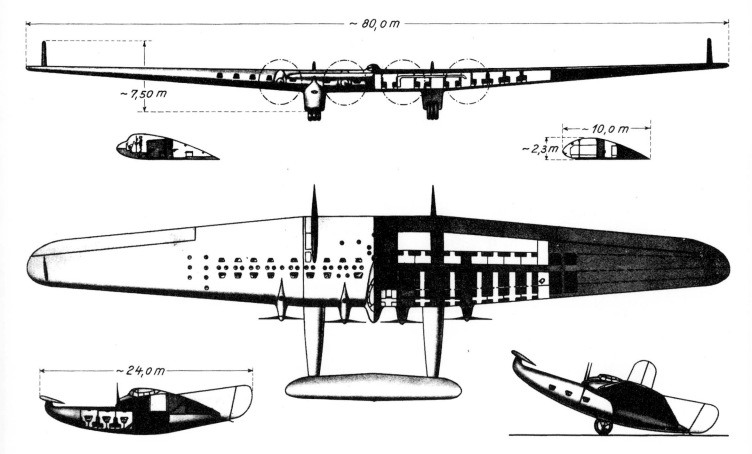

A Dream for the Future

FREQUENTLY in the history of aviation the first great step in a given direction has been, however prophetic, premature. Neither the world nor the industry, tied to contemporary and often conventional methods of construction and to available and sometimes inadequate engines, is usually ready for large leaps forward.

Mention has been made already of Professor Junkers' one great dream, the all-metal aircraft, which he successfully brought to reality. In his other, and vaster, dream – the flying wing – he was never entirely to succeed.

As far back as 1910 Junkers took out a patent for a flying wing. J.W. Dunne had been experimenting with tail-less aircraft with sharply swept wings since 1908 in his search for total inherent stability; but his engine, fuel tank and crew were contained in a conventional nacelle mounted on the lower wing. The whole point of the Junkers patent was that everything, crew, engines, fuel, passengers or payload, should be contained within the wing.

This was logical, but far ahead of its time. The only point of the drag-producing, weight-penalizing fuselage was to carry at its extremities the control surfaces that had been proved to be necessary. If some other aerodynamic solution could be found to control problems, it could be swept away. Unfortunately, even today, this solution has not been completely formulated; ironically, Northrop, the great American protagonist of the flying wing, is now engaged in doing away with the wing, in lifting-body research for NASA.

Junkers produced several further projects for flying wings in the 1920s, all on the grand scale and including the 262-foot span J1000 of 1921. In 1929 he actually built an aircraft that was half-way towards his ideal, the G38.

This had a span of 144 feet $4\frac{1}{2}$ inches, and a wing area of 3229 square feet, which gave it a very low wing loading of 16 lb/square foot and kept the landing speed down to below 50 mph. Although a conventional aircraft, with a normal fuselage and tail, it included a number of features that were steps towards the flying wing. The engines were completely buried in the thickness of the wing (5 feet 7 inches at the root), driving their airscrews through extension shafts, and the inboard pair were in fact coupled units, each made up of two Junkers L8 400-hp in-lines, mounted in a V; the outer engines were single L8s.

Access to the engines for maintenance was possible in flight, and the oil and water radiators were housed inside the wing, being extended into the airflow as required. Six of the thirty-four passengers were also accommodated in the leading edge of the wing, with forward windows. One of the advanced ideas provided for in the patents covering the G38 was a roomy underfloor freight hold beneath the passenger cabin, extending its full length. The object of this arrangement, the patent explained, was to absorb shock in the event of a crash landing removing the undercarriage.

Two G38s were built, the second serving for many years with the German airline, Lufthansa.

Hugo Junkers died in 1935, and his great dream died with him.

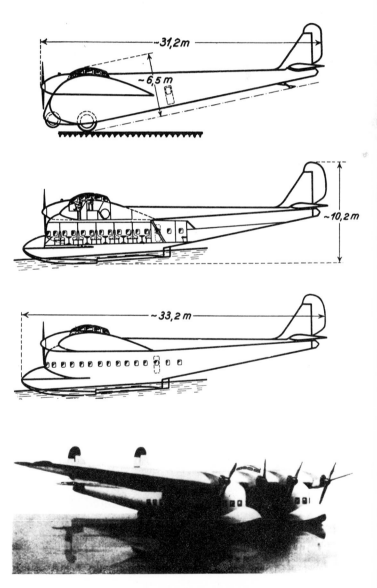

Three years before the J 1000 project, Junkers was working on this four-engined sixty-passenger flying boat and landplane.

Airline Revolution

THE early years of the growth of air transport in the United States have been referred to already. The key to successful operation was the award of a Post Office contract for mail carrying, and by the end of the period under review the major portion of the lucrative routes, covering the coast-to-coast network for the most part, was in the hands of a "big four" of rival airlines.

The four had grown to maturity by a process of acquisition of smaller lines as each strove to control a complete coast-to-coast network. In this they had been helped considerably by the efforts of the Postmaster General, Walter Brown, who believed that the future lay with a few powerful airlines, and awarded contracts carefully to achieve this end. This was to lead to a considerable outcry when the contracts came up for renewal in 1930, but when the dust died down, pretty well the same big four were in control.

The four giants were United Air Lines, Eastern Air Lines, Transcontinental and Western Air (TWA) and American Airlines. United was basically Boeing, to which had been added, among others, Stout Air Services, who had been pioneers of all-passenger services with the popular and comfortable Ford Trimotor. Stout had actually given up their airmail contract because, with the Ford, passengers were

a good deal more profitable.

Boeing themselves, with the Mailplane and the later three-engined Model 80, had begun to cater for passengers at an early stage, and when, after a classic take-over battle, United acquired National Air Transport (NAT), they not only had the last sector of the prize New York-San Francisco route in their hands, they had also obtained a fleet of excellent aircraft with it.

National, like many other airlines in the second half of the 1920s, had initially bothered very little with passengers. It should be remembered that, as each airline developed its own route, any passenger facilities at terminals would have to be provided by the line—a considerable extra expense.

However, the success of the reliable and luxurious Ford Trimotors had increased interest in passenger carrying, and following Lindbergh's epic transatlantic flight, public interest in air travel had itself snowballed, raising the US in world statistics from the status of a minor to a major user of commercial aircraft.

It was the announcement in 1929 that NAT intended to equip with a fleet of the new luxury Curtiss Condors that made them a desirable prize and a potential threat to United—as well as the fact that it was part of the Keys airline empire and Keys' Transcontinental Air Transport formed part of rival TWA.

Left *Three famous American airliners of the late 1920s in front of the Santa Monica control building. On the right, the Ford all-metal Trimotor, on the left the luxurious Curtiss Condor. Above, Boeing's Model 80, another renowned passenger-carrier. Painting by John Young.*

Below *In 1925 Ryan Airlines made history with a year-round service flown with these Ryan-Standard J1s.*

Croydon airport in the 1920s, by Kenneth McDonough. Here we see an Air Union LeO "Golden Ray" airliner and the smaller Bréguet 280.

This Boeing Model 40A gives an early indication of Boeing's interest in catering for people – it carried two passengers as well as mail.

The Boeing Model 200 Monomail pioneered low-wing, retractable-gear, all-metal commercial aircraft.

The Man from Seattle

THE name of Boeing looms large in the history of aviation in the United States. From the requirement issued by the Post Office in 1925 for a replacement for its ageing DH4s, came the Boeing Model 40. This was duly bought by the Post Office, but they failed to come through with any further production order.

Two years later the Post Office relinquished the transcontinental airmail route to individual enterprise and Boeing, interested in the San Francisco–Chicago section, revived the Model 40. This time they had the use of the Pratt and Whitney Wasp radial, considerably lighter than the equal power Liberty of the original model. They therefore not only significantly increased the performance of the aircraft, but were able to include space for two (later four) passengers.

Their low bid from the expected economy of the Wasp and the revenue from passengers gained them the route.

In 1930 Boeing came up with another single-engined mail carrier, this time with no passenger accommodation, but with a number of radically new features. The Model 200 Monomail was powered by a new version of that same Pratt and Whitney, the Hornet, giving 575 instead of 420 hp, and carefully enclosed in an airflow-smoothing cowl. The entire aircraft was of metal, with fully canti-lever wings, removing the drag of wire bracing and struts; the undercarriage retracted into the underside of the wing, leaving half the wheel showing (which was likely to save considerable damage to the structure in the event of a forced landing).

The maximum speed of the 8000-lb aircraft was 158 mph. For all that, the pilot still sat in an open cockpit.

The Monomail gave Boeing designers and engineers a chance to familiarize themselves with the new techniques of metal construction and retracting gear, but it remained a proto-type. This familiarity speeded production of the next significant Boeing design, the Model 215. The 215 was a twin-engined, low-wing bomber with retractable landing gear, stemming obviously from the Monomail. While it was a great improvement over existing bombers, and a small batch was built for the Army, the Martin company came up with a private venture of their own that was a step further ahead, with enclosed cockpits and turrets for the gunners. With this they received the production order that Boeing had hoped for.

The significance of the Boeing B-9 (service designation of the Model 215) was that it was developed into the Model 247, the first modern, clean, monoplane airliner in history. But the story of the 247 is outside this book.

Reaching for Space

FINALLY, we return once more to Germany, for the most prophetic step of all. Fritz von Opel was a car manufacturer who had become interested in the possibilities of rocket propulsion through contact with Max Valier, a publicity-minded member of the *Verein für Raumschiffahrt* (Society for Space Travel).

After a series of more or less successful experiments with cars propelled by Sander powder rockets, Opel himself was the pilot of a test flight in the Hatry Flugzeug rocket glider, Rak-1. The flight took place at Rebstock, near Frankfurt, on September 30, 1928. Power was provided by sixteen of Friedrich Wilhelm Sander's powder rockets,

producing 50 lb of thrust each. The flight was a success, the Rak-1 reaching a speed of 95 mph.

It was not, incidentally, the first flight by a rocket-propelled aircraft, though it was to be the last for some thirteen years. The first rocket glider, built by the *Rhön-Rossiter Gesellschaft,* was flown at the Wasserkuppe, a famous German soaring site, on June 11, 1928. It covered three-quarters of a mile in just over a minute, powered by two slow-burning Sander rockets.

Fritz von Opel, pioneer German rocket car experimenter, flew this rocket glider, Rak-1, successfully on September 30, 1928, but abandoned the experiment after that one flight. An impression by Roger Gould.